Student Handbook to Economics

Macroeconomics

Volume II

Student Handbook to Economics

Macroeconomics

Volume II

JANE S. LOPUS

An Infobase Learning Company

Student Handbook to Economics: Macroeconomics
Copyright © 2013 Jane S. Lopus

Facts On File, Inc.
An Imprint of Infobase Learning
132 West 31st Street
New York NY 10001

Library of Congress Cataloging-in-Publication Data
Student handbook to economics.
    v. cm.
  Includes bibliographical references and index.
  Contents: v. 1. Microeconomics / Julia A. Heath — v. 2. Macroeconomics / Jane S. Lopus — v. 3. International economics / Jane S. Lopus — v. 4. History of economic thought / David Bourne — v. 5. Entrepreneurship / William Smith.
  ISBN 978-1-60413-992-1 (alk. paper) — ISBN 978-1-60413-994-5 (alk. paper) — ISBN 978-1-60413-993-8 (alk. paper) — ISBN 978-1-60413-995-2 (alk. paper) — ISBN 978-1-60413-996-9 (alk. paper) — ISBN 978-1-60413-997-6 (alk. paper) 1. Economics—Handbooks, manuals, etc. 2. Microeconomics—Handbooks, manuals, etc. 3. Macroeconomics—Handbooks, manuals, etc. 4. International economic relations—Handbooks, manuals, etc. 5. Entrepreneurship—Handbooks, manuals, etc. I. Heath, Julia A.
  HB171.5.S9247 2012
  330—dc23
                          2012019189

Facts On File books are available at special discounts when purchased in bulk quantities for businesses, associations, institutions, or sales promotions. Please call our Special Sales Department in New York at (212) 967-8800 or (800) 322-8755.

You can find Facts On File on the World Wide Web at http://www.infobaselearning.com

Text design by Erika K. Arroyo
Cover design by Takeshi Takahashi
Composition by EJB Publishing Services
Cover printed by Yurchak Printing, Landisville, Pa.
Book printed and bound by Yurchak Printing, Landisville, Pa.
Printed in the United States of America

This book is printed on acid-free paper.

CONTENTS

What is economics? Even if you do not have a clear definition of economics in mind, you probably have some good ideas regarding what economics is all about. On a personal level, you know that economics involves jobs and income and whether you can afford to buy things that you want. If you are running a business or plan to do so, economics involves concerns such as costs, revenues, profits, and how to start or expand your business. On a national level, economics looks at issues such as the overall levels of prices, unemployment, and economic growth. Economics also involves international issues such as trade and exchange rates. Some people are under the impression that economics is only about the study of money. Economists do study money, but economics includes much more than this.

The basic economic problem is scarcity. Scarcity exists because economic resources are limited, but people's wants are not. Because of scarcity, we cannot have all of the goods and services that we would like for ourselves and for others, and therefore we have to make choices. Economics is very much about making choices and deciding how to make the best use of scarce resources. With this in mind, we can define economics as a social science concerned with the way society chooses to use its scarce resources to produce goods and services to satisfy people's wants.

The five volumes in our series *Student Handbook to Economics* provide a solid foundation for learning about major topics related to economics and for learning about different approaches to studying economics. *Microeconomics* looks at economics from the viewpoint of individuals, businesses, or industries. It involves studying about supply and demand, or how prices are established in a market economic system. What role the government should play when markets do not work perfectly is another important microeconomic topic.

Macroeconomics looks at economics from the perspective of the whole economy. Macroeconomics addresses problems such as inflation, unemployment, and why the economy has its ups and downs. Macroeconomics also addresses what the government and central bank can try to do about problems in the economy. Our *International Economics* volume investigates topics such as globalization, economic development, trade and trade barriers, exchange rates, and different types of economic systems.

The fourth volume in our economics series, *History of Economic Thought,* takes a historical perspective and traces economic philosophy from Aristotle to the present, addressing the interesting and important topic of the philosophies underlying various economic theories. The fifth volume in our series, *Entrepreneurship*, focuses on the innovative business side of economics. What are the types of business organizations? What is the role of market research? How can you create a company or expand a company? Each of the five volumes provides a framework for better understanding economic topics and issues.

Why is it important to study economics? It is important because it will help you to make better decisions on a personal level. With a better understanding of the world around you, you will be able to make better choices as a consumer and producer or entrepreneur. You will have a better understanding of local, national, and international events and trends covered by the media. You will become a more informed participant in our democracy, and a more informed participant in our global economy. We wish you the best as you embark on your exciting adventure.

CHAPTER 1

INTRODUCTION TO MACROECONOMICS, ECONOMIC SYSTEMS, AND GOALS

Economics is always in the news. A glance at newspaper headlines over time reveals references to inflation, unemployment, banking crises, money, trade deficits, regulation of business, taxes, the national debt, poverty, exchange rates, recessions, expansions, and related subjects. Many of these topics relate to macroeconomics, the subject of this volume. Before we describe what we mean by macroeconomics, it is important to know how we define the study of economics in general and some basic ideas behind the study of economics.

WHAT IS ECONOMICS?

Economics is a social science concerned with how societies choose to use their scarce resources to satisfy people's wants. Economics is a social science because it is concerned with how people behave. Specifically, economics is concerned with how people behave when confronted with the ever-present problem of scarcity. It is human nature that people want more goods and services for themselves and for others. **Scarcity** occurs because there are not enough resources in the world to satisfy these wants. The problem is sometimes described by the saying "Wants are unlimited but resources are scarce." Scarcity is the basic economic problem, faced by all societies. Without scarcity, there would be no need to study economics.

When we study economics, we frequently talk about "the economy." An **economy** refers to the consumption, production, and distribution of goods and services in a certain location. So when we speak about an economy, we are often talking about the economy of a country. But we also use the term to refer to another geographical region, such as part of a country or part of a continent. For example, we could talk about the economy of the San Francisco Bay Area or the economy of Sub-Saharan Africa.

Economic Resources

When we say that resources are scarce, we are generally referring to **economic resources,** which are necessary to produce goods and services. Economic resources are often divided into four categories: land or natural resources, labor, capital, and entrepreneurship. Economic resources can also be called productive resources, factors of production, or just factors. They are sometimes called inputs. In this sense, inputs or resources are used to produce output. For example, land, labor, capital, and entrepreneurship are inputs that go into the production of a car, which is the output.

As an economic resource, **land** refers not just to land itself but to all natural resources or gifts of nature, including trees, oil, wind power, and so on. **Labor** refers to the work of humans in the production of goods and services. Labor results from both physical and mental skills and talents. The work performed by teachers, doctors, truck drivers, and servers in restaurants are all examples of labor.

As an economic resource, **capital** refers to goods that are used to produce other goods that do not get used up in the production process. Capital goods include things like tools, equipment, machinery, and factories. An oven is an example of a capital good because once you have baked bread or a cake, using the oven in the baking process, you still have the oven to produce other goods. Flour would not be a capital good because when you bake the bread or cake, the flour gets used up in the process and you no longer have the flour to produce other goods.

Capital goods are essential for economies to grow and advance, and businesses need to invest in capital goods for economic growth to occur. In fact, in the language of macroeconomics, the word **investment** means spending by businesses on capital goods. If an economy is too poor to save money to invest in capital goods, workers will not have tools and equipment with which to work and it would be difficult for that economy to increase its production of goods and services in the future.

Economic Resources

- Land (natural resources)
- Labor
- Capital
- Entrepreneurship

Factories are examples of capital goods. *(Shutterstock)*

The fourth economic resource is **entrepreneurship**. Like labor, entrepreneurship is a human resource. The word comes from a French word meaning "to undertake." The entrepreneur undertakes risk with the goal of making a profit and organizes the other economic resources to produce goods and services in the best way. Entrepreneurs often have new ideas and start new businesses. There is risk involved because a new business may or may not succeed and earn a profit for the business owners. A business may fail, and the business owners would thus incur losses.

Opportunity Costs and Trade-offs

Referring back to the definition of economics, note that economics is the study of how societies *choose* to use their scarce resources. Because people cannot have everything they want, choices have to be made. Workers have to make choices about what goods and services to buy with their limited incomes, or whether they should save for future spending. Governments have to make choices too, particularly when faced with limited tax dollars and limited borrowing options.

For example, a federal government may have to choose whether it should produce more military goods or spend more on health care.

Every time a choice is made, something is given up. If you have to choose between going to the movies or going to a party and you choose to go to the party, you give up going to the movies. If a local government has to decide whether to spend money on a park or on schools and chooses the schools, it gives up the park. Economists have a term for what is given up when a choice is made: **opportunity cost**. In the examples cited above, the opportunity cost of going to the party was not being able to go to the movies. The opportunity cost of spending on schools was not being able to spend on the park. All choices involve opportunity costs, because all choices mean that something is given up.

A **trade-off**, an economic term that is closely related to opportunity cost, is defined as the exchange of one thing for another. There is a trade-off involved in choosing to go to a party rather than going to the movies, because you have exchanged (or traded off) the opportunity to go to the movies in order to go to the party.

Microeconomics and Macroeconomics
The study of economics is often divided into two categories: microeconomics and macroeconomics. At colleges and universities, it is common to offer separate introductory economics courses specializing in principles of microeconomics and principles of macroeconomics.

Microeconomics is the study of economic decision making by individuals, business firms, and industries. Microeconomics addresses topics such as how prices are determined for specific products, how consumers decide what products to buy and in what quantities, and how producers decide what products to sell and in what quantities. Other microeconomic topics involve decisions by business firms to achieve the goal of maximizing profits. Microeconomics focuses on individual markets and not on the economy as a whole.

Macroeconomics is the study of economic decision making for the whole economy or for major sectors of the economy. The word **aggregate**, meaning total, is often used when talking about macroeconomics. In macroeconomics, we look at aggregate production, the total production for the whole economy, and not just the production of one business firm. In the same way, we look at aggregate income and employment, and not the income or job of an individual. We look at the overall price level for the economy, rather than the prices of individual products.

In some ways looking at the aggregate levels of economic indicators such as income and employment for the whole economy can hide what is happening in certain areas of the country economists are studying. For example, the economy as a whole could be growing or expanding with overall income increasing, but there could be high unemployment and declining incomes in the northeast, due to the decline of certain industries that are located there. However, there are also benefits of looking at the economy from the macro-economic perspective. Looking at aggregate values allows us to see the big picture for the whole economy, and to make comparisons across countries and across time.

ECONOMIC SYSTEMS

Economies can be organized in different ways, and this can greatly affect the lives of the people who live under different economic systems. For example, most people living under Cuba's economic system have vastly different lives compared to those living under the economic system that exists in the nearby U.S. state of Florida. An **economic system** is the way that an economy organizes the ownership, production, and distribution of its economic resources. To better understand this idea, we will look at three basic questions that all economic systems must address and answer. These questions are sometimes referred to as the "what, how, and for whom" questions. The method or way that economies answer these questions will determine what type of economic system they have.

Three Basic Questions All Economic Systems Must Answer

The first question that all economic systems must answer is what goods and services will be produced with their scarce resources. Since no economy can produce everything that everyone wants for themselves and others, decisions must be made about what to produce (and what not to produce). One economy may decide to produce more military goods and fewer consumer goods than another. Another economy may specialize in producing agricultural goods, and another may produce more manufactured goods.

The second question that all economies must answer is how the goods and services will be produced. In most cases, there are different ways to produce things. For example, it may be possible to produce goods with different types of machines or with different combinations of workers and machinery. If you have a lawn-mowing business, you may be able to mow ten lawns a day using

Three Basic Questions

What goods and services will be produced?
How will the goods and services be produced?
For whom will the goods and services be produced?

ten workers and ten push-type lawn mowers or by using two workers and a lawn tractor.

The third question that all economic systems must answer is for whom the goods and services are produced. This question addresses how the goods and services will be distributed, or who is going to end up getting them. Will goods and services be distributed so that everyone has equal quantities of everything? Or will the people who work the hardest get the most? Or will the most needy people get the most?

Types of Economic Systems

To see how economies organize the ownership, production, and distribution of their economic resources, we can look at how they answer the three basic questions discussed above. These answers allow us to classify economic systems as command, traditional, or market economic systems. But it is important to understand that all economic systems are really a mixture of these three basic systems and that a **mixed economic system** comprises some characteristics from all three types of economic systems.

Command

In **command** economic systems, the questions of what to produce, how to produce, and for whom to produce are answered by those in power. Command economies might be run by kings or monarchs, by a controlling political party (such as Cuba's Communist Party), or by whoever controls the government. The decision making about what, how, and for whom is usually **centralized**, meaning that decisions are made by a few powerful people rather than by many private individuals.

The Soviet Union, which existed from 1917 to 1991, had a command economic system. Decisions about what goods and services should be produced and in what quantities were made by central committees of the Communist Party and by centralized ministries. **Ministries** were government organizations in charge of different industries, including steel, agriculture, and machinery. Decisions about production processes (that is, those answering the "how" question), were often made at the ministry level. Thus, distribution of goods and services was decided (in theory) by the central Communist Party with the objective of somewhat equal distribution. In reality, there were vast shortages of consumer goods throughout Soviet history.

Tradition

In economic systems organized by **tradition**, decisions about what goods and services to produce, how to produce them, and how to distribute them are made based on the way things have been done in the past. If you were to ask people in a traditional economy why they were producing certain goods, the response would likely be that these were goods that had been produced by their ancestors. Values based on customs, religion, and culture are important in traditional economic systems.

Although many traditional economic systems that existed in the past no longer exist today, there are still examples of economic systems that are primarily traditional today. Some tribes living in the Amazon rainforest continue to hunt and fish with tools and methods similar to those of their ancestors. The clothing and shelter that they produce and use also follow ancestral traditions.

Market

A **market** is any place where something is bought or sold. In a **market economic system**, individual producers and consumers answer the questions of what, how, and for whom through markets. Sellers decide what goods and services to produce based on what they think buyers want to buy. Because sellers would not want to produce something nobody would buy, the decision about what goods and services will be produced is made by buyers as well as by sellers. In this way, a market economic system generally produces goods and services that consumers want.

In a market system, producers decide how to produce goods and services and have strong incentives to produce them in the most efficient way. **Productive efficiency** means producing goods and services in the least costly way and not wasting any resources. When producers produce goods and services efficiently, they are able to keep their prices down. Competition plays a role here, because if a producer's costs are higher than a competitor's costs, he or she may have to charge higher prices. Assuming all the goods or services were of the same quality, consumers would most likely choose the less expensive goods or services and do business with the competitor. Eventually, the less efficient producer would probably go out of business.

In a market system, the "for whom" question is also answered through markets. People buy the goods and services produced with money they earn from working. The wages and salaries people earn are determined in labor markets, and some earn more than others. For example, those who work cutting grass earn lower salaries than those who work as electrical engineers, partly because there is a much greater supply of people who have the skills to do lawn maintenance than people trained in electrical engineering. As a result of their higher incomes, the engineers would be able to buy more goods and services than the lawn workers.

The United States is largely a market economic system. Most decisions about what goods and services to produce are made by people in private businesses, who pay close attention to what they think buyers will want to buy. Businesses strive to use efficient production methods to keep costs down and to be competitive. People earn money primarily by working, and those who have money

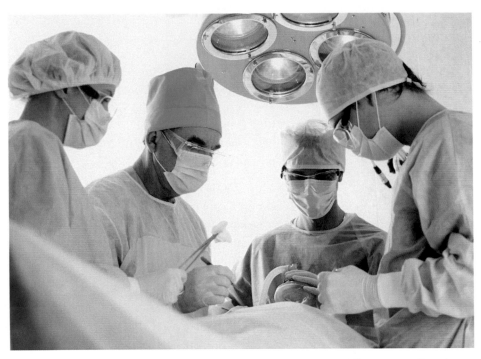

Medical professionals are highly trained individuals with specialized skills, commanding above average salaries in the marketplace. *(Shutterstock)*

can purchase goods and services. It is important to emphasize that in market economic systems, most of the what, how, and for whom decisions are made by individuals or private businesses and not by the government.

ECONOMIC GOALS

Everyone wants the economy to do well. But what does this mean? And how do we evaluate how well the economy is doing? On a personal level, many people might respond that they would like the economy to perform so that they have steady jobs, high incomes, good housing, and enough of the goods and services they would like to make them happy. They may also want more goods and services for others, for example for family and friends or for people in need around the world. Having the economy perform well may also mean having steady and predictable prices. Other goals may involve social issues such as preserving the environment or ensuring that people have a secure retirement income. Another important goal for many people is economic freedom.

To truly understand whether an economy is doing well, it is necessary to have a basic understanding of the economic goals of economies throughout the world. Although there are many differences in emphasis and priorities across countries, there is some agreement about broad social goals for different

Broad Social Goals for Economies

- Economic efficiency
- Economic growth
- Economic stability

- Economic equity
- Economic freedom

economic systems. These goals can be divided into five broad categories: economic efficiency, economic growth, economic stability, economic equity, and economic freedom.

Economic Efficiency
Productive Efficiency

Economists sometimes divide economic efficiency into two subcategories: productive efficiency and allocative efficiency. As noted above, productive efficiency is achieved if we are producing goods and services in the least costly way without sacrificing quality. Achieving economic efficiency means that we are not wasting our scarce economic resources: our land, our labor, our capital, and our entrepreneurship.

Because there are different ways of producing goods and services using different combinations of resources, productive efficiency is achieved by finding the least costly method for producing a certain quantity and quality of output. Say that you could produce a table with two different combinations of labor and capital using the same amount of natural resources. Assume that with either method, you could produce one table in one hour. Because the cost of the natural resources is the same in either case, we need to compare the cost of using the different amounts of labor and capital to see which is most efficient. Table 1.1 presents two potential combinations of labor and capital.

Method 1 utilizes three workers and two machines, while Method 2 utilizes two workers and three machines. Assume that the costs of the workers and machines are the same for both methods, and that all of the workers are equally skilled and the machines are of equal quality. As Table 1.1 shows, Method 2 is more efficient because it is the least costly way to produce the table, given the costs of workers and machines. The cost of three workers and two machines for Method 1 is $55, whereas the cost of two workers and three machines for Method 2 is $45. Some people may consider that Method 2 is not fair to workers because the third worker (not hired using Method 2) would have to find another job. Other people might consider Method 1 not fair to consumers because the higher cost of producing the table would most likely mean a higher purchase price. This is an example of a trade-off between economic goals, which will be discussed later in this chapter.

TABLE 1.1
Inputs and Costs of Producing One Table in One Hour

Costs: One worker = $15 per hour; One machine = $5 per hour		
	Cost	Most efficient?
Method 1 3 workers and 2 machines	3 ($15) + 2 ($5) = $55	
Method 2 2 workers and 3 machines	2 ($15) + 3 ($5) = $45	Method 2 is most efficient because the cost is lower.

Allocative Efficiency

Allocative efficiency occurs when the goods and services produced are those that people in the economy value and are willing to buy. This means that economic resources (land, labor, capital and entrepreneurship) are allocated to the production of the goods people want. For example, if people want more tables and fewer chairs, resources would be allocated to the production of tables. Like productive efficiency, competition helps to achieve allocative efficiency in market economies. Because business firms hope to earn profits and stay in business, they have incentives to produce the goods and services that people want to buy.

Economic Growth

If we want more goods and services for ourselves or for others without taking them away from someone else, we need economic growth. **Economic growth** occurs when more goods and services are produced in one time period than before. Economic growth is usually measured by increases in real **gross domestic product** (GDP), or real **GDP per capita**, over a year. **GDP** is the total amount of final goods and services produced in a given economy in a given year. **GDP per capita** means GDP per person. It is computed by taking the total amount of GDP in a country and dividing that amount by the population. This gives a measure of how much GDP is available for each person in that country, although it does not tell us how GDP is actually distributed. **Real GDP** refers to GDP that has been adjusted for changes in overall prices. Making these price adjustments enables us to have realistic comparisons of changes in GDP and economic growth across time, even if the overall level of prices has changed. GDP will be discussed in more detail in Chapter 2. Economic growth will be discussed in more detail in Chapter 3.

Economic Stability

Economic stability refers to the goal of having a stable economy instead of an economy that fluctuates widely. A stable economy is characterized by steady economic growth, employment, and prices. There is usually a direct connection between economic growth and available jobs: When GDP grows and more goods and services are produced, generally more jobs are available. This does not mean that there is no unemployment or that no one ever gets laid off when an economy is experiencing steady growth. In market economies, demand for products is always changing so employment is also always changing. In the macroeconomic sense, economic stability of employment refers to the idea that jobs are not lost due to overall declines in GDP.

Economic stability also refers to stable prices. **Inflation** occurs when the overall price level is increasing, and **deflation** occurs when the overall price level is decreasing. Price stability is important because it helps people plan for the future. If you are saving for an important purchase such as a house and prices are increasing in unexpected ways, you are not likely to know how much you need to save.

Economic Equity

The word *equity* means fairness. The goal of **economic equity** means that we want the economy to be fair. On the surface this seems simple and straightforward, because no one would want an economy to be unfair. But different people have different opinions about what is fair and what is not. For example, is it fair for the government to promise a minimum wage to workers? A worker may say yes, but an employer who has to pay higher wages to the worker may say no. Is it fair to raise local taxes to make more money available for public schools? Your answer may depend on whether you or your children attend or attended a public school or a private school. And what about people who have no children, or who no longer have children in school? These are just two examples illustrating that economic equity can be controversial and that fairness means different things to different people. Other real-life examples are all around you.

It is important to underscore that the word *equity* refers to fairness and not necessarily to equality. Equity does not guarantee that everyone will receive an equal amount of income, for example. Nor does it guarantee that all goods and services will be equally accessible to everyone unless a society decided that a more equal distribution of goods and services were fair or equitable. Many people, however, believe that distributing income equally would be neither fair nor equitable, because they also believe that those who work harder or who have more (or more specialized) skills or talents should be paid more than an unskilled person or someone who chooses not to work hard.

Economic Freedom

On an individual level, **economic freedom** refers to the right to make your own choices about what to consume, what to produce, what education to pursue, what career to pursue, and whether to start your own business or work for someone else. When you live in a country like the United States, which has a high level of economic freedom, it is sometimes easy to take these freedoms for granted. Imagine what it was like to live in the Soviet Union when decisions about housing, education, and careers were often made by the government rather than by individuals and families.

There are organizations that measure economic freedom and its impact on other goals in different countries. One of these organizations is the Heritage Foundation (www.heritage.org). The Heritage Foundation publishes the Index of Economic Freedom each year. Using ten measures of freedom (including business freedom, investment freedom, labor freedom, and property rights), the Heritage Foundation ranks over 180 countries by an economic freedom score. In 2011 the United States ranked ninth in the world on this scale. Many people believe that economic freedom is an important goal for an economy because higher economic freedom is often associated with more success in achieving other goals, such as economic growth and economic stability.

Countries with Highest Economic Freedom, 2011

RANK	COUNTRY
1	Hong Kong
2	Singapore
3	Australia
4	New Zealand
5	Switzerland
6	Canada
7	Ireland
8	Denmark
9	United States
10	Bahrain

Source: Heritage Foundation: www.heritage.org

Priorities Among Economic Goals

How important is each of the economic goals to an economy? That depends on the priorities of those making the economic decisions. For example, the command economy of the former Soviet Union placed a low priority on economic freedom and a high priority on economic stability and economic growth. In the long run, the methods used to try to achieve stability and growth were not successful and the Soviet Union collapsed in 1991. Today many of the former Soviet countries have transitioned to become market-based systems.

Market economic systems place a high value on economic freedom and especially on the freedom to own property. Market systems also value economic efficiency. Some critics of market systems point to unequal distribution of resources and large differences between rich and poor people, saying that there is not enough emphasis on equity.

Trade-offs Among Economic Goals

Most people would probably agree that all of the economic goals are important. So why do economies sometimes have trouble achieving them? Part of the answer to this question will be addressed in future chapters when we look at economic growth, inflation, and unemployment in more detail, and part of the answer depends on the role of the government and central bank in addressing these goals. But part of the answer also has to do with trade-offs between the goals. Sometimes working to achieve one goal conflicts with another goal. Some examples of trade-offs between the goals follow.

If you value economic stability, you want people to be able to have steady jobs. But as our example about producing a table showed, this may conflict with economic efficiency. In our example, it was more efficient to use more machines and fewer workers, so the worker who was not hired would have had to look for another job. There was, therefore, a trade-off between employment stability for the worker and productive efficiency.

Another example would be a trade-off between economic equity and economic growth. You may think that it is fair or equitable to require a steel mill to buy equipment to reduce air pollution emitted during the production of steel. But if the business had to buy this equipment, it may mean that it could not afford to purchase other resources (such as labor or electricity) necessary to produce steel. In this case, it could not produce as much steel. If the decreased production due to anti-pollution regulations were widespread and not offset by the increased production of pollution equipment, this could mean less economic growth. This could also reduce employment in the steel industry, which would create a conflict with economic stability.

There are many similar trade-offs between economic goals, resulting in situations where achieving one goal means giving up achieving another goal. These trade-offs often limit the ability of an economy to achieve all of the desirable economic goals at the same time. Decisions about how to resolve these trade-offs are often made in the political arena.

SUMMARY

Economics investigates how people respond to the problem of scarcity, because economic resources are scarce relative to people's wants. Macroeconomics deals with issues faced by the economy as a whole. It includes GDP, growth, business cycles, and the role of the government and central bank in stabilizing the economy. All economic systems must address basic questions about what, how, and for whom goods and services are produced. In evaluating the performance of an economy, it is helpful to think of goals that the economy may pursue. Many of these goals are related to efficiency, growth, stability, equity, and freedom. Different types of economic systems may decide to prioritize different goals. There are often trade-offs between the goals, so that they cannot always be achieved simultaneously.

Further Reading

Gregory, Paul R., and Robert C. Stuart. *Comparing Economic Systems in the Twenty-First Century.* 7th ed. Houghton Mifflin Company: Boston, 2004.

2011 Index of Economic Freedom. Heritage Foundation. Retrieved online September 2011 at www.heritage.org/Index.

CHAPTER 2

MEASURING ECONOMIC PERFORMANCE: GROSS DOMESTIC PRODUCT

One way to measure how well an economy is doing is to measure the total amount of goods and services produced in a country in a certain time period, such as a year. Economists use gross domestic product (GDP) to measure the production of an economy. But how do we measure GDP? And if prices change over time, how can we compare GDP from year to year? Moreover, is GDP a good measure of the well-being of people in an economy? These are some of the questions that will be addressed in this chapter.

WHAT IS GDP?
Gross domestic product, often abbreviated as GDP, is the total market value of all of the final goods and services produced in an economy in a certain time period. In reporting GDP, the area involved is usually a country, although GDP can also be reported for a region of a country or for a group of countries. The time period involved is usually a year, although GDP figures for the United States are also reported quarterly, or every three months. In the United States, GDP is calculated by the Bureau of Economic Analysis or the BEA, which is part of the U.S. Department of Commerce (www.bea.gov).

The U.S. economy produces a great many different things, including apples, bacon, shoes, computers, airplanes, services provided by nurses and teachers, and so on. So how can we compile all of these very different things into a single GDP? One way to do this is to add together the amount spent for different goods and services, or to add together their **market value.** Thus, we add together the amount spent on apples, the amount spent on bacon, the amount spent for nurses' services, and the amount spent on other goods and services. In theory, we do this for all the final goods and services produced in the country in a given year.

It is important to underscore that the definition of GDP refers to **final goods and services** because GDP measures the value of goods and services at the prices paid by the final consumers. This allows us to avoid counting some things twice. For example, if we counted the value of the windshield added to a new car as well as the sales price of the new car, we would be counting the value of the windshield twice, because it is already part of the value of the car. Thus a windshield is an example of an intermediate good. An **intermediate good** is an item used in the production of final goods and services. By including only the market value of final goods and services and excluding intermediate goods and services, we avoid counting the value of the intermediate goods twice.

An alternative way to measure GDP is to use a value-added approach. Instead of using the value of final goods and services in GDP, the **value-added approach** sums up the amount added to the value of the product at each stage of production. By adding the increased value at each stage of production, the amount is equivalent to using the value of final goods and services.

In addition to intermediate goods, several other categories of goods and services are not included in GDP. Some of these are listed in the sidebar below. If goods and services are produced but not sold in the marketplace, then they are not included in GDP. If, for example, you cut your own grass, this is not included in GDP. But if you hire a gardener to cut your grass, that would be included in GDP. GDP also excludes transfer payments. A **transfer payment** is a payment made to someone for which no goods or services were currently produced in return. Social Security payments, unemployment insurance payments, and dividends earned from owning stock are examples of transfer payments. GDP does not include the value of used goods. It includes only new goods and services produced during the given time period. If you buy a new car, the price

What Goods and Services Are Not Included in GDP?

- Intermediate goods and services
- Good and services not sold in the market place
- Transfer payments
- Used goods
- Purely financial transactions
- Illegal goods and services

Used goods, such as those typically found at garage sales, are not included in a nation's GDP. *(Shutterstock)*

of the car would be included. If you buy a used car, the price would not be included. GDP also excludes the value of purely financial transactions such as the purchase of stocks and bonds. The production of illegal goods and services is not included in GDP. Because illegal goods and services are traded in the "underground" economy, these transactions are not included in GDP, although some people do estimate the value of certain illegal transactions, such as the illegal drug trade.

GDP and GNP

The definition of GDP refers to the goods and services produced within a country's borders. This is where the "domestic" part of gross domestic product comes from. It is important to understand that the goods and services produced in a country are included in calculating GDP, even if they were produced by a company owned by people from a different country. For example, if the Swedish company Ikea produces goods in the United States, these goods are considered part of U.S. GDP. But if the American company Ford produces cars in Mexico, the value of the production is not considered part of U.S. GDP.

Gross national product, or GNP, measures production by foreign companies in a different way. **Gross national product** is the market value of all final

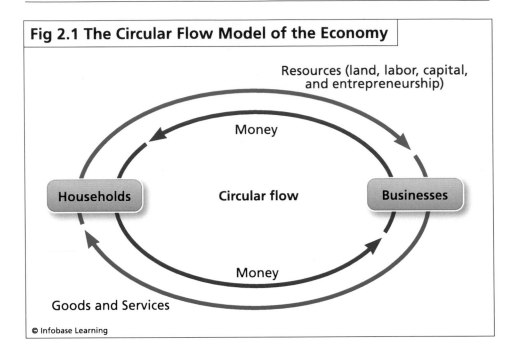

Fig 2.1 The Circular Flow Model of the Economy

Resources (land, labor, capital, and entrepreneurship)

Money

Households   Circular flow   Businesses

Money

Goods and Services

© Infobase Learning

goods and services produced by the residents of a country, either within the country or in another country. U.S. GNP would include the value of Ford production in Mexico, but would not include the value of Ikea production in the United States. Before 1991, the United States used GNP as its official measure of total production. It switched to using GDP, partly to make production measurement consistent with that of other nations of the world, who more often use GDP as their official measure of production.

The Circular Flow of Economic Activity

A circular flow diagram of the economy provides a good way to visualize GDP. The diagram in Figure 2.1 shows the flows of goods and services, resources, and money between businesses and households. The bottom flow shows goods and services produced by businesses going to households. In exchange, households pay money to businesses for the goods and services they buy. You can think of this money flow as representing GDP, because it shows the dollars spent on goods and services produced in the economy.

The top two flows in the circular flow diagram illustrate the flow of economic resources (land, labor, capital, and entrepreneurship) from households to businesses. In this diagrammed flow, we are assuming that households own all of the resources and sell them to businesses. The top money flow represents the income that households receive in exchange for selling resources. For example, when you go to work for a business, you sell your labor to the business in exchange for wages. In this simple economy, the amount of this income flow will be equal to the GDP money flow in the bottom of the diagram. This simple circular flow does not include flows to and from the government sector, the foreign sector, or the financial sector of the economy. However the simple two-sector model is sufficient to show the ideas behind GDP and national income

HOW DO WE MEASURE GDP?

The circular flow diagram can be used to show two different approaches to measuring GDP. We can measure GDP by the money flow on the bottom of the circular flow, which represents spending on the final goods and services produced in the country in a year. This is the expenditures approach to measuring GDP. Or, we can measure GDP by the income flow at the top of the circular flow. This is the income approach to measuring GDP. This section examines these two approaches in more detail.

Expenditures Approach to Measuring GDP

When the BEA measures GDP, it totals spending on goods and services in four major categories: consumption, investment, government purchases, and net exports. This can be expressed by the following formula:

$$GDP = C + I + G + Xn$$

Table 2.1 shows total U.S. GDP for five selected years broken down into these four major categories.

Consumption

In GDP accounts, consumption is called Personal Consumption Expenditures. Column three of Table 2.1 lists Personal Consumption Expenditures for the years 1970, 1980, 1990, 2000, and 2010. Consumption includes household spending on goods and services. Goods include tangible things that you buy, such as food, textbooks, and bicycles, whereas services include things that others do to help you, like getting your teeth cleaned at the dentist's office or having food served to you in a restaurant. Goods can be classified as durable or non-durable. **Durable goods** are goods that will last for three or more years with normal usage. **Non-durable goods** are those that wear out in less than three years with normal usage. Examples of consumer durable goods are washing machines and cars. Food and clothing are examples of non-durable goods. Note that the purchase of a new house is added to investment rather than to consumption when measuring GDP.

TABLE 2.1

U.S. GDP: Selected Years (Billions of current dollars)

Year	GDP	Personal Consumption Expenditures (% of total)	Gross Private Domestic Investment (% of total)	Government Consumption Expenditures and Gross (gov't) Investment (% of total)	Net Exports of Goods and Services (% of total)
1970	1,038.3	648.3 (62%)	150.4 (14%)	233.7 (23%)	4.0 (.40%)
1980	2,788.1	1,755.8 (63%)	485.6 (17%)	566.1 (20%)	−13.1 (−.50%)
1990	5,800.5	3,835.5 (66%)	846.4 (15%)	1,181.7 (20%)	−77.6 (−.01%)
2000	9,951.5	6,830.4 (69%)	1,717,7 (17%)	1,731.0 (17%)	−382.1 (−4%)
2010	14,660.2	10,351.9 (71%)	1,752.8 (12%)	3,002.3 (20%)	−515.5 (−4%)

Source: Economic Report of the President, http://www.gpoaccess.gov/eop/ Table B-1. Figures for 2010 are preliminary. Percentages computed from totals shown. GDP totals do not equal the sum of the components due to rounding errors. Percentages may not total 100% due to rounding errors.

Investment

Investment is called Gross Private Domestic Investment and includes spending on capital goods, which are used to produce more goods and services in the future. It also includes spending on residential and non-residential structures and spending on equipment and software. You may wonder what happens to GDP if a business produces a good but no one buys it. The good ends up in business inventories, and the investment part of GDP also includes changes in business inventories. This is important to understand, because changes to inventories can affect future business decisions about how much to produce. Changes to business inventories can either be planned or unplanned.

Why is investment called Gross Private Domestic Investment? In this case, the word "gross" means total. Here "gross" refers to the fact that spending on both new and replacement investment goods is included. In other words, if a computer wears out and is replaced with another, this spending is included in gross private domestic investment and in GDP. "Private" refers to the fact that the investment spending counted here is from the private sector of the economy and does not include government investment spending. And "domestic" means that the investment spending took place within the United States.

Government Purchases
The government component of GDP consists of government spending on goods and services by all levels of government: federal, state, and local. It consists of both consumption and investment spending by government. The federal section can be broken down into defense and non-defense spending. The government spending included in GDP is not the same as total government spending because it does not include government transfer payments, as such payments do not represent spending for current production.

Net Exports
Net exports refers to spending on exports minus spending on imports. **Exports** are goods and services produced in the United States and sold to people in other countries. **Imports** are goods and services produced in other countries that are purchased by people in the United States. Spending on U.S. exports is included in U.S. GDP because it represents production that took place in the United States. However, spending on imports is not included in GDP because it represents production in other countries.

Comparing GDP Expenditures of the U.S.
If you take another look at Table 2.1 you will likely notice that GDP has increased from 1970 to 2010, from $1 trillion to over $14 trillion. We will discuss these amounts in more detail later in this chapter. Another thing you may notice is that consumption is the largest part of GDP for each of the years shown and has grown as a percentage of GDP over time.

Investment is the third largest component of GDP. Although the absolute amount of investment is higher in each subsequent year shown, it did not increase very much between 2000 and 2010. This is likely due to the recession that occurred between January 2008 and June 2009. Government purchases of goods and services, the second largest component of GDP, averages 20 percent of GDP for the years shown.

The last column in Table 2.1 shows negative numbers for net exports from 1980 through 2010. These numbers are negative because for every year since the mid-1970s, the United States has spent more on imported goods than people in other countries have spent on U.S. exports. This means that the United States has a **trade deficit**. This trade deficit accounted for about 4 percent of GDP from 2000 through 2010.

Measuring National Income

The circular flow diagram presented earlier in the chapter shows two money flows: the flow of spending on goods and services (the expenditures approach to measuring GDP) and the flow of spending to purchase resources used in producing goods and services. In our simple two-sector circular flow model, these two money flows are equal. Spending equals income, because when you pay money to buy something, that money becomes income to someone else. The flow of spending to purchase resources provides a measure of income to those who supply economic resources: land, labor, capital, and entrepreneurship. This represents national income. **National income** is the sum of rent, wages and salaries, interest, and profits, including proprietors' incomes. It also includes taxes on production and imports. National income represents the income paid to people who supply the resources to produce goods and services.

Table 2.2 shows the breakdown of national income in 2010. Rent consists of payments made to households and businesses that rent property. Wages and

TABLE 2.2
U.S. National Income, 2010 (Billions of current dollars)

1	**National Income**		**$13,082.70**
2	Rent	$308.40	
3	Wages and salaries	$8,100.30	
4	Interest	$730.60	
5	Profits:		
6	Corporate profit	$1,678.30	
7	Proprietors' income	$1,080.20	
8	**Total: Rows 2, 3, 4, 6, 7**		**$11,897.80**
9	Taxes on production and imports	$1,072.70	
10	Other statistical adjustments	$112.20	
11	**Total: Rows 8, 9, 10**		**$13,082.70**

Source: www.bea.gov.

salaries are the largest component of national income and represent payments to people who supply labor. Interest includes the interest households and businesses receive on their savings, less the interest they pay to borrow. This includes the interest businesses pay when they borrow to buy capital goods. Profit includes the profits that corporations earn, plus income that proprietors earn. **Proprietors** are people who own their own businesses.

Note that when we add up rent, wages and salaries, interest, and profits, they do not quite total national income. National income also includes taxes on production and imports and other statistical adjustments to arrive at the total of $13,082,700,000 shown at the end of Table 2.2. Taxes on production and imports represent spending, but the money spent goes to the government. For example, if you buy a notebook that is priced at $5 in a state that has a seven percent sales tax, you will pay $5.35 for the notebook. Five dollars will go to the seller, and thirty-five cents will go to the government.

Other Related Income Accounts

So far, we have looked at GDP, GNP, and national income. Three additional accounts of interest are net national product (or net domestic product), personal income, and disposable personal income. The relationship between these income and product accounts is shown in Table 2.3. The first row of the table shows GDP in 2010. The next two rows make the adjustments from GDP to GNP, by adding in the value of production of U.S. businesses in other countries and subtracting the value of production of foreign companies in the United States.

Net National Product

Net national product (NNP) is what is left over after depreciation of capital goods has been subtracted from gross national product (GNP). **Depreciation** occurs when capital goods wear out. For example, tools, factories, computers, and other capital goods suffer from wear and tear, or depreciate, over time. The value of this depreciation is estimated and called "consumption of fixed capital" in the national income and product accounts. In the same way, **net domestic product** (NDP) is found by subtracting depreciation from gross domestic product. NNP and NDP are informative because they tell us the value of new goods and services being produced in the economy, after the value of replacement capital goods has been subtracted. NNP and NDP only include the value of new additions to the stock of capital goods.

Personal Income

Although national income is an interesting measure of the contributions to production from different types of resources, it does not tell us how much we potentially have to spend. For this, the BEA computes personal income. **Personal income** is the income people receive from all sources. This means that

TABLE 2.3

The Relationship Between Income and Product Accounts, 2010 (Billions of current dollars)

Gross Domestic Product	**$14,871.4**
Plus: Income receipts from the rest of the world	730.8
Less: Income payments to the rest of the world	552.8
Gross National Product	**$15,049.3**
Less: Consumption of fixed capital (depreciation)	1,890.7
Net National Product	**$13,158.6**
Less: Statistical discrepancy	130.0
National Income	**$13,028.7**
Less: Income earned but not received (e.g., payroll deductions for Social Security)	4,557.4
Plus: Income received but not earned (e.g., welfare and other transfer payments)	4,252.7
Personal Income	**$12,724.0**
Less: Personal taxes*	**$1,359.3**
Disposable Personal Income	**$11,364.7**

Source: Bureau of Economic Analysis, National Income and Product Accounts.
*Computed from BEA Table SA51-53 and Table 1.7.5

some things have to be subtracted from national income and some things have to be added to national income to arrive at personal income. For example, the contributions from a worker's paycheck that go toward Social Security are part of national income because they are part of the income that the worker earned. But because the worker does not actually have that money to spend, these contributions are not part of personal income. On the other hand, transfer payments are considered part of personal income but not part of national income. This is because transfer payments such as unemployment compensation or interest earned represent personal income that a person has and can spend, but cannot be considered national income because it is not paid to people for supplying resources to produce goods and services.

Disposable Personal Income

Personal income still does not quite tell you exactly how much you have to spend, because you have to pay personal taxes. **Disposable personal income** is personal income minus current personal taxes. In other words, it is how much income you have available to either spend or save after you have paid your taxes. This may be the figure that is most important to you in making decisions about your current and future consumption and savings patterns. Of course, figures for the whole country are averages and cannot be specifically applied to your own situation.

REAL VERSUS NOMINAL GDP

One of the nice things about knowing GDP and the related accounts for a country is that it allows us to see how the production of final goods and services has changed over time. But looking at GDP measured in current dollar prices for different years can be misleading if prices have changed over time. A simple example illustrates this problem and shows how economists resolve this problem. Assume that we are looking at a country called Econia. The people in Econia produce only one good: chairs. The number and price of chairs produced in two hypothetical years, 2000 and 2010, are shown in the sidebar below.

In the Year 2000, Econia produced 100 chairs that sold for a price of $10 each. **Nominal values** are values measured in current prices. Therefore, in the year 2000, nominal GDP was $1,000 ($10 × 100 chairs). In 2010, 150 chairs were produced and sold for a price of $20 each. Nominal GDP in 2010 was $3,000 ($20 × 150 chairs). If all we know is nominal GDP, it appears that GDP has tripled between 2000 and 2010. We can see, however, that part of this increase was due to prices increasing from $10 to $20 per chair during this period, and not because three times as many chairs were produced.

Economists compute real GDP to take into account price changes over time. **Real values** are values that have been adjusted for changes in prices. To find real GDP, we need to select a base year. A **base year** is a year that is used to compare

Output and Prices for the Country of Econia

	Chairs Produced	Price of Chairs	Nominal GDP
Year 2000	100	$10	$1,000
Year 2010	150	$20	$3,000

If 2000 is the base year, then real 2010 GDP (in 2000 prices) = $1,500 (150 x $10)

how much prices have changed over time. In our example, we will select 2000 as the base year. Real 2010 GDP is then found by taking the quantity of goods and services produced in 2010 and multiplying that quantity by the prices that were in existence in the base year. Real 2010 GDP with 2000 as the base year is equal to $1,500 (150 chairs times $10). This gives us an accurate reflection of how much actual production changed from the base year to the current year, holding prices constant. Computing real GDP taking into account all the goods and services produced in a country and all the different prices is of course more complicated than in this simple example, but the example roughly shows how it is done.

Table 2.4 shows U.S. nominal and real GDP for selected years from 1965 to 2010. The base year is 2005. In the base year, nominal GDP is equal to real GDP because the current 2005 prices are used. In the years after 2005, nominal GDP is greater than real GDP because prices were higher than in 2005.

TABLE 2.4
U.S. Nominal and Real GDP: Selected Years
(Base year = 2005)

Year	Nominal GDP (Billions of dollars)	Real GDP (Billions of chained 2005 dollars*)
1965	719.1	3,610.1
1975	1,637.5	4,879.5
1985	4,217.5	6,849.3
1995	7,414.7	9,093.7
2005	12,638.4	12,638.4
2006	13,389.9	12,976.2
2007	14,061.8	13,228.9
2008	14,369.1	13,228.8
2009	14,119.0	12,880.6
2010	14,660.2	13,248.7

Source: 2011 Economic Report of the President, Table B-1 and B-2.
*"Chained dollars" result from a statistical process that links changes in prices over time.

Real GDP takes these price changes into account by using a measure of 2005 prices. If we look only at nominal GDP, it looks like production increased more than it really did. In the years before 2005, real GDP is greater than nominal GDP. This is because prices were higher in 2005, the base year, than in the years shown. Computing real GDP using 2005 prices allows us to compare the level of actual production in years before and after the base year.

IS GDP A GOOD MEASURE OF ECONOMIC WELL-BEING?

GDP (and real GDP when prices are changing) is a fairly good measure of the total production of goods and services in an economy. We say "fairly good" because we have to remember that goods and services that are produced but not sold in the marketplace and illegal transactions are not included in GDP. Sometimes GDP is used to indicate not only how much is produced in an economy but how well off people are in an economy. This can be valid in the sense that having more goods and services is usually better than having fewer goods and services. But there are several things to consider before we use GDP as a measure of how well off people are. Some of these things are listed in the sidebar.

A country's GDP tells you about the amount of goods and services produced, but it does not tell you how the goods are services are distributed. Per capita GDP, or GDP per person, gives you a better idea of how many goods and services are available for each person in a country. For example, assume that Country A and Country B both have GDP of $5 billion, but County A has a population of one million and Country B has a population of five million. In this case per capita GDP would be $5,000 in Country A ($5 billion / 1 million) but $1,000 in Country B ($5 billion / 5 million). Per capita GDP tells you how many goods and services are available for each person if the goods and services were evenly distributed, but it still does not tell you how the goods and services are actually distributed. For example, it could be that one group of people is able

Problems with Using GDP as a Measure of Well-being

- Does not account for distribution of output
- Does not account for value of leisure
- More is not always better
- Does not address spending on crime and other "bads"
- Does not account for changes in product quality

to keep most of the goods and services for itself and that most of the people in the country have very little.

Another problem with using GDP as a measure of well-being is that it does not take into account the value of leisure time. To illustrate this problem, assume that two people graduated from the same college with degrees in economics and had the same job prospects when they left college. One of these people now chooses to spend most of his time surfing and hanging out on the beach with his friends. He supports himself by working part time as a waiter earning $20,000 per year. The other person earns $200,000 a year in a high-pressure job as an investment banker. She works long hours during the week and on weekends and cannot easily leave her job to take vacations. The first person contributes $20,000 to GDP, and the second contributes $200,000 to GDP. Is the second person necessarily ten times better off? The surfer may value his leisure time and unpressured lifestyle, even though he is not contributing as much to GDP. The investment banker may be contributing more to GDP but may be chronically tired and stressed out.

Another example can also be used to show that generating more goods and services does not necessarily mean that people are better off. For example, say that one worker lives across the street from her office and walks to work. Another worker drives his car to the train station, takes the train to the city, and then takes a bus to his office. The first worker's commute contributes nothing to GDP while the second worker's commute contributes to GDP from the use of the car, train, and bus. Probably most workers would prefer the short commute even though this would contribute less to GDP than the longer commute.

A related issue is that because GDP is a measure of total output, it includes the value of the production of things that we would perhaps rather do without. For example, people who are afraid of crime in their neighborhood may purchase guns to protect themselves or put bars on their windows. These purchases increase GDP. GDP also goes up when the government spends money to house criminals in prison. It would no doubt be better if there were no crime in the first place and these expenditures did not occur, even though GDP would be lower. In addition to spending on crime, GDP includes spending on other "bad" things, such as spending for cleaning up damage to the environment caused by the production and consumption of goods and services.

Another reason why increases in GDP do not always mean that people are better off is that over time, improved technology and production methods result in higher quality and lower-priced products. For example, laptop computers were more expensive ten years ago than they are today, and they also had fewer capabilities and features. Although the more expensive computer added more to GDP than the cheaper and more powerful computer today, you are clearly better off with today's computer.

SUMMARY

Because gross domestic product measures the value of the final output of goods and services in an economy, it is an important measure of how an economy is doing. We can measure GDP by looking at spending on goods and services or by looking at income flowing to economic resources. Other accounts related to GDP include gross national product, net national product, national income, personal income, and disposable personal income. When overall prices are changing, looking only at the current levels of GDP can be misleading. Therefore we can distinguish between nominal GDP and real, or inflation adjusted, GDP. Although GDP is an important measure of production, it is not a perfect measure of the well-being of the population in a country. We will revisit the idea of GDP in the next chapter when we look at economic growth, and in Chapter 4, when we address the ups and downs of economic activity.

Further Reading

A Guide to the National Income and Product Accounts of the United States. Bureau of Economic Analysis. Available online. Accessed May, 2011 at http://www.bea.gov/national/pdf/nipaguid.pdf.

An Introduction to the National Income and Product Accounts. September, 2007. BEA: U.S. Department of Commerce. Available online. Accessed April 2011 at http://www.bea.gov/scb/pdf/national/nipa/methpap/mpi1_0907.pdf.

Bureau of Economic Analysis, U.S. Department of Commerce. www.bea.gov

Economic Report of the President: 2011 Report Spreadsheet Tables. Available online, Accessed 5/2011. http://www.gpoaccess.gov/eop/.

National Income and Product Accounts, Bureau of Economic Analysis. Available online. Accessed 5/20/11 at http://www.bea.gov/national/nipaweb/TableView.asp?Selected Table=43&FirstYear=2010&LastYear=2011&Freq=Qtr.

CHAPTER 3

ECONOMIC GROWTH

Economic growth is a widely held goal for nations around the world. When economies grow, more goods and services are available, leading to increased standards of living for the population. How do we know if the economy is growing and how fast it is growing? GDP, discussed in Chapter 2, helps us to answer these questions. Economic growth is often defined as an increase in real (inflation adjusted) GDP over some time period, such as a year. It is also defined as an increase in real GDP per capita, or per person, over some time period. Why is economic growth important? What are factors that lead to economic growth? How do we measure economic growth? What do we know about economic growth rates in different countries? These are some of the questions that are addressed in this chapter.

WHY IS ECONOMIC GROWTH IMPORTANT?
President Kennedy referred to economic growth as a "rising tide that lifts all boats." What this means is that economic growth can improve the material living standards for low-income, middle-income, and high-income individuals. When economic growth occurs, more goods and services are produced. When economic growth is measured as an increase in per capita GDP, this means that more goods and services are available for everyone. These goods and services can improve people's well-being. In wealthy countries, economic growth can benefit people by providing access to new, improved, and a wider variety of goods and services. For the poorest people in the world, economic growth can

provide access to clean water, sanitation, nutritious food, medicine, and medical services. Of course economic growth does not always benefit everyone, nor does it ensure that everyone will benefit equally. How goods and services are distributed within an economy can vary greatly.

Production Possibilities Model

A **production possibilities model** provides a way to visualize economic growth by showing potential combinations of two goods that can be produced with a given amount of resources. Figure 3.1 is an example of a production possibilities model showing possible combinations of consumer goods and capital goods that a hypothetical economy could produce with its resources. First look at the solid curve marked for the year 2000. The economy can produce different combinations of consumer and capital goods indicated by all of the points on this curve (such as points A, B, C, or D) if it uses its resources efficiently. Which point the economy chooses depends on the preferences of the people in the economy and the type of economic system it utilizes.

In the year 2000, because of scarce resources, this economy cannot produce quantities of consumer and capital goods indicated by point E. Point E is outside of the production possibilities curve for 2000 and represents an unattainable point. However, if the economy experienced economic growth, it could have more resources to produce more consumer goods and more capital goods in

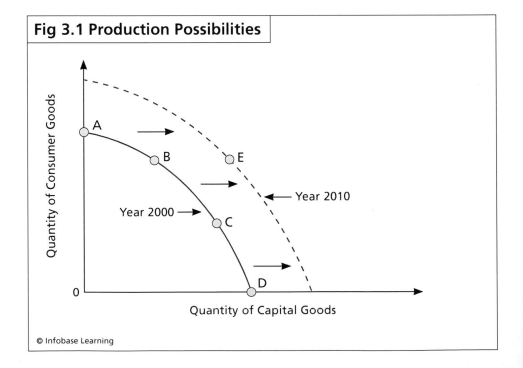

Fig 3.1 Production Possibilities

Quantity of Consumer Goods

Quantity of Capital Goods

Year 2000

Year 2010

© Infobase Learning

a future year. Economic growth can be shown as an outward shift of the production possibilities curve, from the solid curve to the dotted curve in Figure 3.1. The dotted curve represents production possibilities in 2010 after economic growth has taken place. Economic growth would enable the economy to produce the quantities of goods indicated by point E, or other combinations on the new, higher production possibilities curve. If the economy began at point C in 2000, there would be both more consumer goods and more capital goods at point E in 2010.

Economic Growth Through History

During much of human history and until about 200 years ago, economic growth throughout the world was accompanied by increases in population. When more goods and services were produced, making more food available, the population would increase. Per capita income therefore did not change very much. Table 3.1 shows changes in GDP per capita through history. From about 5000 BC

TABLE 3.1
World Economic Growth Through History

Year	Population*	GDP per Capita**
−5000 BC	5	$130
1000 BC	50	$160
1	170	$135
1000	265	$165
1500	425	$175
1800	900	$250
1900	1625	$850
1950	2515	$2,030
1975	4080	$4,640
2000	6120	$8,175

*Millions
**In year 2000 international dollars.
Source: J. Bradford Delong: The Reality of Economic Growth: History and Prospect, pg. 2. http://www.j-bradford-delong.net/macro_online/ms/ch5/chapter_5.pdf.

through 1500 AD, real GDP per capita ranged from about $130 to $175. Beginning with the Industrial Revolution, the world's per capita income began to rise dramatically. Many inventions, such as the printing press, steam engine, and better ways to make cloth, improved people's lives and led to increased production and economic growth.

Economic growth has not been even throughout the world. Over the past 200 years, the United States and Western European countries have experienced higher economic growth than most other parts of the world and now have higher per capita GDP than most other parts of the world. Over time, growth rates are inconsistent within countries also. For example, Figure 3.2 shows the growth rates of real GDP for the United States from 2004 to 2010. We can see that over this time period, GDP increased by as much as five percent from the prior quarter, but it also decreased by almost seven percent in the fourth quarter of 2008. Reasons for short-run fluctuations in GDP will be explored in Chapter 4.

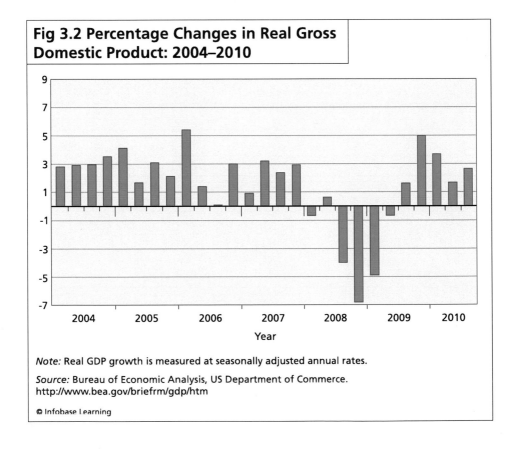

Fig 3.2 Percentage Changes in Real Gross Domestic Product: 2004–2010

Note: Real GDP growth is measured at seasonally adjusted annual rates.

Source: Bureau of Economic Analysis, US Department of Commerce. http://www.bea.gov/briefrm/gdp/htm

© Infobase Learning

Benefits of Economic Growth

Economic growth has many benefits to people. If you have any doubts about this, think about the goods and services that are available to you today compared to those available to people in the United States in 1850, when even the wealthiest people did not have a car, a computer, a refrigerator, a telephone, a television, or air conditioning. They could not take a plane to visit another country and they could not watch a movie. The quality of medical care was much lower in 1850 than today, regardless of how much money someone had. Economic growth has led to improvements in technology that have greatly increased the quantity and quality of goods and services available to most Americans today. This is part of what we mean when we say that economic growth leads to increases in the standard of living. **Standard of living** gauges how well off people are in terms of the goods and services they have, as well as other measures of well-being, such as life expectancy and access to education and health care.

Table 3.2 shows standard of living indicators for selected countries and provides insights into how economic growth can affect the well-being of people in different countries. The first column lists ten selected countries that range from having relatively high GDP per capita to having very low GDP per capita. The countries are listed from the highest to lowest levels of GDP per capita. Higher GDP per capita indicates more economic growth in the past. The next three columns report data about the quality of life in the ten countries. Infant mortality rates and life expectancy are indicators of health and medical care available within the countries. For the most part, Table 3.2 shows that countries with higher GDP per capita have lower rates of infant mortality and higher life expectances. There are exceptions, but these overall trends are quite clear. The last column shows the expected level of schooling for the selected countries. More education is correlated with higher levels of GDP per capita. And when children remain in school longer, there is less child labor, another benefit of economic growth.

While discussing the benefits of economic growth, we should also mention that economic growth can have harmful side-effects, such as a detrimental impact on the environment. It is easy to picture a large factory causing air and water pollution while it produces more goods and services and jobs for people. Negative environmental effects can be addressed with proper incentives and regulations. Overall, the benefits to growth far outweigh the costs.

FACTORS CONTRIBUTING TO ECONOMIC GROWTH

Many different things have led to economic growth across time and in diverse locations. But despite these differences, we can identify factors that are helpful

TABLE 3.2
Standard of Living Indicators (selected countries)

Country	GDP per capita	Infant Mortality Rate (deaths per 1000 live births)	Life Expectancy at Birth	Expected Years of Schooling
United States	$47,200	6.1	78.4	16
Sweden	$39,100	2.7	81.0	16
Japan	$34,000	2.8	82.3	15
Argentina	$14,700	10.8	77.0	16
Turkey	$12,300	23.9	72.5	12
China	$7,600	16.1	74.7	11
Armenia	$5,700	18.9	73.2	12
Ghana	$2,500	48.6	61.0	10
Chad	$1,600	95.3	48.3	7
Afghanistan	$900	149.2	45.0	8

Source: Columns 1–4 CIA World Factbook Country Comparisons. Column 5 from United Nations Statistics Division: Demographic and Social Statistics.

and sometimes necessary for economic growth to occur. A good way to begin is to look at the role of the basic factors of production: natural resources, capital resources, and human resources.

Sources of Growth: Economic Resources
Natural Resources
Although it is helpful to have natural resources, it is not necessary for a country to have large quantities of natural resources in order to have economic growth. Some countries have had rapid economic growth despite a lack of economic resources. Examples include Japan after World War II and more recently, Singapore and Hong Kong. Moreover, just because countries have many natural resources does not ensure that they will experience rapid economic growth and become wealthy. Certainly vast natural resources have helped the United States and Canada reach the levels of income that they have today. But the same has not been true for African nations such as Kenya.

Capital Resources

For a nation to grow, it has to be able to produce more goods and services than are necessary for consumption. If a country consumes everything it produces (for food and shelter for example), it will not be able to save any income to produce capital goods. Saving and investing in capital goods are necessary for economic growth, because capital goods such as tools, factories, and machinery are used to produce other goods and services in the future.

Look again at Figure 3.1 showing the Production Possibilities Model. Say that two countries both begin with the initial production possibilities shown by the solid line in the year 2000. Country B begins at Point B and Country C begins at Point C. Other things remaining the same, which country would you expect to grow faster in the future? The answer is Country C. Because it is producing more capital goods in 2000 than Country B, we can expect that it will be able to produce more goods (capital or consumer) in the future when compared to Country B.

However, focusing on producing capital goods is not enough to ensure economic growth. During its 80 year history, the Soviet Union tried to focus on the production of capital goods over consumer goods to obtain high economic growth. But both output and income fell in the 1980s, and the Soviet system collapsed by the early 1990s. This helps to show that how investment takes place is also important.

Human Resources

Humans make many contributions to economic growth. Labor is the largest economic resource in most economies, and labor-force participation is important for economic growth. The **labor force participation rate** is the percentage of the working-age population that is working or looking for work. When a larger percentage of the population is working, this contributes to economic growth. Note that increases in the labor force participation rate are different from increases in the entire population. If an economy's population is growing too rapidly and people are not working productively, it can be difficult to support the population and maintain a high level of GDP per capita. Many low-income nations have rapid population growth rates.

The quality of the labor force is important, as well as the number of workers. Economists use the term **human capital** to mean the knowledge, skills, and training that people acquire in schools or on the job. As you acquire education, training, or job experience, you are investing in human capital. A more educated, skilled, and experienced labor force contributes to economic growth. A review of the countries in Table 3.2, which lists standard of living indicators, shows that countries with the lowest per capita incomes are those with the lowest expected years of education.

When workers are more educated, skilled, and experienced, they are more productive. **Productivity** is the amount of output that results from a unit of input in a certain time period such as an hour. **Labor productivity**, also called worker productivity, is the output that results per hour that people work. For example, if ten workers work three hours each and produce 30 cars, labor productivity is one car per hour (30 cars divided by 30 hours worked). If ten workers work two hours each and produce 60 cars, labor productivity is three cars per hour (60 cars divided by 20 hours worked).

There are several things that contribute to higher labor productivity. Three of the main factors are listed in the sidebar below. Investing in human capital through education and training makes workers more productive because as they acquire more knowledge and skills they are able to perform their jobs more quickly and more efficiently. When workers have more and better capital goods with which to work, they are also able to produce things more quickly and more efficiently.

The ratio of capital to labor is an important component of labor productivity. Imagine the labor productivity in an office where ten workers share one computer and then compare this to the productivity in an office where ten workers each have their own computers. The quality of capital is also an important determinant of labor productivity. Imagine the productivity of an agricultural worker farming with a simple hoe, and now compare this to the potential productivity of a worker who has modern agricultural machinery.

Technological advances relate to the quality of capital goods and have been very important in contributing to worker productivity and economic growth. Historically, technological advances stemming from inventions such as the printing press and assembly line have led to great increases in worker productivity. In recent decades technological advances affecting computers and software have greatly improved business efficiency and worker productivity. Communication and access to information from the Internet and the telecommunications industry will likely continue to improve productivity. Advances in medical research improve health, and this also leads to increased labor productivity.

What Makes Workers More Productive?

- Education and Training
- Quantity and Quality of Capital
- Technological Advances

Technological advances can often be easily transferred to poorer, developing countries. When foreign companies build advanced factories in developing countries, local workers are likely to benefit from higher wages than they would otherwise earn. The foreign-built factories and other businesses can help increase productivity and lead to economic growth in developing countries. Knowledge and information spread via the Internet and computers can also be easily transferred to poorer countries.

Sources of Economic Growth: Incentives and Institutions

Looking at how economic resources affect economic growth identifies many important sources of growth but does not tell the whole story. Economics involves how people respond to incentives, and incentives can affect economic growth. An **incentive** is something that encourages people to act in a certain way. For example, if your boss tells you that you will get a big raise if you work harder, you would have an incentive to be more productive. If you have an idea for a new invention and you expect that you may earn a lot of profit from this invention, you would have an incentive to develop the product.

Some countries have institutions that give entrepreneurs incentives to develop and expand businesses that lead to economic growth, whereas other countries do not. In this context, **institution** means an organization that is devoted to promoting a specific cause. An institution does not have to be a physical place such as a building; it can be a custom or system of beliefs. Some examples of institutions that provide incentives that lead to economic growth are listed in the sidebar below.

Economic freedom includes the rights of people to buy and sell what they want, to study what they want, and to work where they want. It includes the right to participate in choosing the government and a limited role of government in making decisions for people. It includes the right to trade with people from other countries. Economic freedom involves the right to compete, to start a business, and to invest freely. Economic freedom also involves freedom from

Institutions That Provide
Incentives for Economic Growth

- Economic Freedom
- Market-based Economic System
- Property Rights
- Stable Political System
- Stable Financial System

government corruption. As discussed in Chapter 1, one well-known index of economic freedom is published by the Heritage Foundation (http://www.heritage.org/Index/). There are strong correlations between high GDP per capita and countries that have high degrees of economic freedom, and vice versa.

Market-based economic systems are related to economic freedom. In a market-based system, the role of government is limited and producers and consumers decide what, how, and for whom to produce goods and services. Properly functioning market-based economic systems provide incentives for producers to go into businesses that will produce the goods and services that consumers are willing and able to purchase. This promotes economic growth.

Property rights and the protection of property rights are important components of market-based economic systems. Clearly defined and enforceable property rights give people incentives to start and expand businesses, which lead to economic growth. For example, if you are thinking of starting a business in a foreign country, you would want to chose a country where you were not afraid that the government would soon take over your business. Countries with enforceable property rights are more likely to experience economic growth than those without enforceable property rights. Having a legal system that enforces contracts between people is another institution related to property rights and can help protect property rights.

For countries to attract foreign and domestic investment projects that lead to economic growth, they should have stable political and financial systems. There would not be strong incentives to invest in a country where the government was expected to fall in the near future or where it was unclear as to how governmental power would be passed on to the next leader. Stable financial institutions such as banks and stock exchanges can help to channel money from those who save to those who want to borrow. This can also promote economic growth.

MEASURING ECONOMIC GROWTH

We have seen that economic growth can be defined as an increase in real GDP, or as an increase in real GDP per capita over a time period. Using per capita GDP to measure economic growth gives us a better measure of whether or not more goods and services are available, on average, for individuals. For example, if real GDP was growing in a country but the population was growing faster, then per capita GDP would be falling.

Economic growth is often expressed in terms of percentage changes or a growth rate. Figure 3.2, discussed earlier, shows percentage changes in U.S. real GDP for different quarters (three-month periods) between 2004 and 2010. It is easier to compare growth rates between countries and within countries in different time periods by looking at percentage changes rather than looking at dollar amounts of changes in GDP.

The rate of growth for real GDP can be computed by using the following formula, which pertains to any percentage change:

Growth rate of real GDP = Change in real GDP / Original GDP

For example, real GDP in the United States was $10,779.8 billion in 1999 and $11,226.0 in 2000 (*Economic Report of the President* 2011). What was the rate of growth of real GDP over this year? Using the formula above, the answer is 4.1 percent (11,226 - 10,779.8 = 446.2 / 10,779.8).

The **Rule of 72** is a mathematical formula that can be applied to economic growth rates (and other percentage changes) and allows us to make some interesting observations. This is how it works: Take the number 72 and divide it by the growth rate of real GDP for a country. This will tell you how long it will take for real GDP to double. For example, if China's real GDP is growing at about 10 percent per year, we would expect China's real GDP to double in about 7.2 years (72/10). If Austria's GDP is growing at 2 percent per year, we would expect Austria's real GDP to double in 36 years.

Growth Rates of Real GDP for Selected Countries (annual rates adjusted for inflation)

China	10.3%
Philippines	7.3%
Hong Kong	6.8%
Indonesia	6.1%
Chile	5.3%
Russia	4.0%
Algeria	3.3%
United States	2.8%
Belgium	2.0%
Iraq	0.8%
World Average:	4.9%

Source: CIA World Factbook Country Comparison, 2010

Robert Lucas, who won the Nobel Prize in Economics in 1995, wrote the following about economic growth: "The consequences for human welfare involved in questions . . . (about economic growth) are simply staggering: Once one starts to think about them, it is hard to think about anything else." The previous sidebar reports the real GDP growth rates for 10 selected countries. You can use these figures and the Rule of 72 to approximate how long it will take GDP to double in these countries. The Rule of 72 shows us that economic growth can help poorer countries catch up with richer countries. Of course if a country is starting with very low levels of GDP, it can take a long time for it to catch up with rich countries. But because poor countries can benefit greatly from improved education, technology, and capital goods, economic growth is a key to improved standards of living and better lives in the future.

SUMMARY

Economic growth leads to increased standards of living for people because it results in increased production of goods and services. A production possibilities model can be used to show economic growth. Economic growth, as measured by increases in real per capita GDP, has increased greatly since the Industrial Revolution. However, growth has been uneven across time and across countries. The quantity and quality of capital and human resources are important for economic growth and can lead to higher productivity. A country's institutions, such as economic freedom, property rights, and a system of markets, also help to promote economic growth. Using the Rule of 72, we can see that economic growth can help poor countries to catch up to the higher income levels of wealthier countries.

Further Reading

CIA World Factbook Country Comparisons. Retrieved online June 2011 at www.cia.gov.

Delong, J. Bradford. "The Reality of Economic Growth: History and Prospect." Retrieved online June 2011 at http://www.j-bradford-delong.net/macro_online/ms/ch5/chapter_5.pdf

John F. Kennedy Quotations. John F. Kennedy Presidential Library & Museum. Retrieved online June 2011 at http://www.jfklibrary.org/Research/Ready-Reference/JFK-Quotations.aspx

Lucas, Robert E. "On the Mechanics of Economic Development." *Journal of Monetary Economics* 22 (1988): 3–42.

Real GDP 1962–2010. *Economic Report of the President 2011.* Retrieved online June 2011 at http://www.gpoaccess.gov/eop/2011/xls/ERP-2011-table2.xls.

Real GDP, Percent Change. Bureau of Economic Analysis. U.S. Department of Commerce. Retrieved online June 2011 at http://www.bea.gov/briefrm/gdp.htm.

United Nations Statistics Division: Demographic and Social Statistics. Retrieved online June 2011 at http://unstats.un.org/unsd/demographic/products/socind/education.htm.

CHAPTER 4

BUSINESS CYCLES: THE UPS AND DOWNS OF THE ECONOMY

Economies have their ups and downs. Sometimes the economy does well: Employment is high, prices are stable, businesses grow, and people's incomes rise. At other times, the economy is not doing so well. Unemployment is high, prices are unpredictable, economic growth slows down, and people's incomes fall. Economists use the term **business cycle** to describe these recurring fluctuations in economic activity. What happens during different phases of the business cycle? What is the history of business cycles in the United States? Why do business cycles occur? These are some of the questions discussed in this chapter.

THE PHASES OF THE BUSINESS CYCLE

Business cycles have occurred over and over in the United States and throughout the world, but no two business cycles are exactly the same. We can, however, identify different phases of a typical business cycle, and common characteristics of each phase. Figure 4.1 is a diagram of a typical business cycle. Economic activity, which includes real GDP, is presented on the vertical axis, and time is presented on the horizontal axis. Because business cycles last for different lengths of time, we do not specify a certain number of years on the horizontal axis. The figure identifies four phases of the business cycle: expansion, peak, contraction or recession, and trough. The upward sloping dotted line indicates that economies grow over time, despite the downward phases of the cycles.

In the United States, the National Bureau of Economic Research (NBER: www.nber.org) is the organization that officially determines when business

Fig 4.1 The Business Cycle

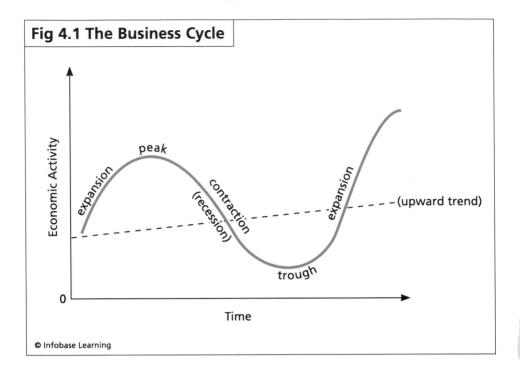

© Infobase Learning

cycles occur. The NBER is a private, non-profit, non-partisan research organization founded in 1920 to promote a better understanding of how the economy works. The Business Cycle Dating Committee, part of the NBER, is the key player in establishing official business cycle dates. The NBER looks at increases and decreases in overall economic activity to establish business cycle dates. The organization does not have a set definition of economic activity. Economic activity includes measures of employment and real GDP from both the income and product approaches. It may also include other indicators, such as sales and industrial production.

Expansion

In the expansion phase of a typical business cycle, real GDP increases and unemployment falls. Incomes and consumption of goods and services rise. Because there is an increase in business sales, business investment in capital goods also increases. Businesses expand. If the economy approaches full employment, there may be a tendency for prices to rise. Expansions are periods of optimism for consumers and producers. Individuals and businesses are willing to borrow for large purchases. Interest rates, the cost of borrowing money, may rise along with prices. According to the NBER ". . . during an expansion, economic activity rises substantially, spreads across the economy, and usually lasts for several years" (www.nber.org/cycles/recessions.html). In Figure 4.1, the expansion is shown where the curve measuring economic activity is increasing over time.

Peak

The peak of the business cycle marks the end of the expansion. It is the turning point where the economy begins contracting. This phase is shown in the figure as the top of the business cycle, where economic activity is at its highest point after the expansion. As the economy approaches the peak, it may be nearing full employment and producing as much as possible. For this reason, inflationary pressures are often associated with the peak of the business cycle. Inflation is a sustained increase in the average of all prices.

Because the peak is a turning point, there are often warning signs of the contraction to come. Business inventories may begin to build up. **Inventories** are the stock of goods that have been produced but that have not been sold. If businesses have more goods in inventories than they planned, they will decrease production in the future, which will lower future employment. Business sales may begin to decline. Overall, employment may not decrease during the peak, but there are signs of things to come. For example, people who have been working overtime may lose their overtime hours and overtime pay. Businesses that used to struggle to fill orders may now find that they are caught up.

Contraction

In the contraction phase of the business cycle, economic activity is decreasing. In the figure, this is shown where the curve representing economic activity is falling over time, from the peak to the trough. Because GDP is declining and fewer goods and services are produced than in the past, some people lose their jobs and unemployment increases. Wages and incomes fall, and so does consumption. Investment declines as businesses do not purchase new capital goods. Prices may fall during contractions, or the rate of inflation may slow. There may also be downward pressure on interest rates as people and businesses borrow less. During contractions, people are often pessimistic about the future outlook of the economy.

Recessions

The NBER defines a **recession** as "a significant decline in economic activity spreading across the economy, lasting more than a few months, normally visible in real GDP, real income, employment, industrial production, and wholesale-retail sales (www.nber.org/cycles.html). A recession is the period between a peak and trough of economic activity. But there may also be a contraction of very short duration (within a period of expansion) that would not be considered a recession. At times the news media and some textbooks define a recession as two or more consecutive quarters of declining real GDP. Although most recessions officially declared by the NBER do meet this definition, this is not the official NBER definition of a recession.

Depressions

A **depression** is a severe recession. The NBER does not identify or date depressions, and there are no set rules for when a recession becomes a depression. Today the term depression is generally used in the United States to refer to the Great Depression of the 1930s. During the Great Depression, economic activity peaked in August 1929 and then contacted for 43 months until the trough in March 1933. Another 13-month contraction took place from May 1937 through June 1938. Real GDP fell about 27 percent from 1929 to 1933, about five times more than in recessions occurring after World War II. The Great Depression is often seen as having ended in 1940–1941 with the buildup of war spending to support the country's involvement in World War II.

This 1931 photograph shows a breadline in Boston during the Great Depression, the most severe economic crisis in U.S. history. *(Library of Congress)*

Trough

The trough is the lowest point in the business cycle. It is shown by the bottom part of the curve in Figure 4.1. When an economy is in the trough phase, GDP has fallen to a relative low point. Unemployment is high. Wages and incomes have declined, resulting in a related decrease in consumption. Business investment is relatively low. However, like the peak, the trough is a turning point. During the trough, there may be some signs that the economy is improving. For example, because capital goods wear out over time, some businesses need to replace them. This helps to increase production levels. Lower prices are also likely to encourage spending on goods and services. Low interest rates may encourage borrowing.

After the trough, as the economy begins to improve, an expansion begins. Because the economy is seen to be recovering from the prior recession, economists and the news media often refer to the period following the trough as a recovery rather than an expansion. In September 2010, for example, the NBER announced that a trough had occurred in June 2009, marking the end of the recession that began with the peak in December 2007. In July 2011, a year after the trough, GDP growth remained low (1.9 percent) and unemployment remained high (9.2 percent). Therefore the economy was said to be experiencing a slow recovery rather than an expansion.

Differing Effects of Business Cycles

Although looking at trends and characteristics of the different phases of business cycles for the overall economy can be revealing, it is important to realize that these trends and characteristics do not always reflect what is happening to each individual, family, or business. We sometimes lose sight of the fact that business cycles affect people differently. For example, in a recession, some people are hired or promoted, and their incomes rise accordingly. Conversely, during an expansion, some people get laid off and some businesses fail. Sometimes when the overall economy is expanding, certain parts of the country can experience economic contraction. And when the overall economy is contracting, certain parts of the country may experience regional growth, including the emergence of new industries.

BUSINESS CYCLES IN U.S. HISTORY

The NBER maintains a record of business cycles that have occurred in the United States since December 1854. This record is shown in Table 4.1. The first column lists the dates of business cycle peaks, and the second column lists the dates of business cycle troughs. The number of months for the contraction, the period from the peak to the trough, is presented in the third column. The length of expansions in months is given in column four. It is interesting to note that

(continues on page 52)

TABLE 4.1
U.S. Business Cycle Expansions and Contractions

BUSINESS CYCLE REFERENCE DATES		DURATION IN MONTHS			
Peak	Trough	Contraction	Expansion	Cycle	
Quarterly dates are in parentheses		Peak to Trough	Previous Trough to This Peak	Trough from Previous Trough	Peak from Previous Peak
	December 1854 (IV)	—	—	—	—
June 1857 (II)	December 1858 (IV)	18	30	48	—
October 1860 (III)	June 1861 (III)	8	22	30	40
April 1865 (I)	December 1867 (I)	32	46	78	54
June 1869 (II	December 1870 (IV)	18	18	36	50
October 1873 (III)	March 1879 (I)	65	34	99	52
March 1882 (I)	May 1885 (II)	38	36	74	101
March 1887 (II)	April 1888 (I)	13	22	35	60
July 1890 (III)	May 1891 (II	10	27	37	40
January 1893(I)	June 1894 (II)	17	20	37	30
December 1895 (IV)	June 1897 (II)	18	18	36	35
June 1899 (III)	December 1900 (IV)	18	24	42	42
September 1902 (IV)	August 1904 (III)	23	21	44	39
May 1907 (II)	June 1908 (II)	13	33	46	56
January 1910 (I)	January 1912 (IV)	24	19	43	32
January 1913 (I)	December 1914 (IV)	23	12	35	36
August 1918 (III)	March 1919 (I)	7	44	51	67
January 1920 (I)	July 1921 (III)	18	10	28	17
May 1923 (II)	July 1924 (III)	14	22	36	40
October 1926 (III)	November 1927 (IV)	13	27	40	41

| BUSINESS CYCLE REFERENCE DATES | | DURATION IN MONTHS | | | |
| Peak | Trough | Contraction | Expansion | Cycle | |
Quarterly dates are in parentheses		Peak to Trough	Previous Trough to This Peak	Trough from Previous Trough	Peak from Previous Peak
August 1929 (III)	March 1933 (I)	43	21	64	34
May 1937 (II)	June 1938 (II)	13	50	63	93
February 1945 (I)	October 1945 (IV)	8	80	88	93
November 1948 (IV)	October 1949 (IV)	11	37	48	45
July 1953 (II)	May 1954 (II)	10	45	55	56
August 1957 (III)	April 1958 (II)	8	39	47	49
April 1960 (II)	February 1961 (I)	10	24	34	32
December 1969 (IV)	November 1970 (IV)	11	106	117	116
November 1973 (IV)	March 1975 (I)	16	36	52	47
January 1980 (I)	July 1980 (III)	6	58	64	74
July 1981 (III)	November 1982 (IV)	16	12	28	18
July 1990 (III)	March 1991 (I)	8	92	100	108
March 2001(I)	November 2001 (IV)	8	120	128	128
December 2007 (IV)	June 2009 (II)	18	73	91	81
Average, all cycles:					
1854–2009 (33 cycles)		16	42	56	55
1854–1919 (16 cycles)		22	27	48	49
1919–1945 (6 cycles)		18	35	53	53
1945–2009 (11 cycles)		11	59	73	66

* 32 cycles
** 15 cycle
Source: NBER: www.nber.org/cycles.html

(continued from page 49)

for the business cycles that have occurred since World War II, expansions have been getting longer on average and contractions have been getting shorter on average. The last two columns in the table show the length of the 33 business cycles that have occurred since 1854, when measured from trough to trough (or 32 cycles if measured from peak to peak).

Although the average length of a business cycle occurring since 1854 is about 4.6 years (55–56 months), very few cycles have lasted exactly this long, and the duration has varied extensively during this period. The longest expansion (120 months) took place from March 1991 to March 2001, and the longest contraction (65 months) took place from October 1873 to March 1879. The shortest expansion (10 months) took place from March 1919 to January 1920, and the shortest contraction (6 months) took place from January 1980 to July 1980.

The NBER's Business Cycle Dating Committee issues statements on the current state of the business cycle. These are widely quoted in the press and are available through a link on the NBER homepage (www.nber.org). As of July 2011, the most recent statement relating to the business cycle was made in September 2010 when the NBER reported that a trough had occurred in June 2009, ending the recession that began in December 2007 and beginning an expansion.

CAUSES OF BUSINESS CYCLES

There are many different theories about causes of business cycles. In this section, we will take a brief look at some of the more common ideas about why business cycles occur. As you might imagine, it would be preferable to have steady, predictable economic growth and avoid the inflationary pressures associated with business cycle peaks and the unemployment problems associated with troughs and contractions. What the government and central bank can do to try to address the problems of the business cycle will be discussed in Chapters 6 and 8.

Aggregate Demand and Aggregate Supply

The level of GDP and the overall price level in an economy are determined by aggregate (total) demand and aggregate (total) supply. Therefore, understanding why fluctuations occur in real GDP, employment, and other factors affecting overall economic activity is perhaps easier when viewed in terms of aggregate demand and aggregate supply. Figure 4.2 shows a model for aggregate demand and short-run aggregate supply. In macroeconomics, the **short-run** is the time period when all markets have not adjusted to their equilibrium levels because wages or other input prices are not totally flexible. When the economy has reached equilibrium in the short run, aggregate demand is equal to short-run

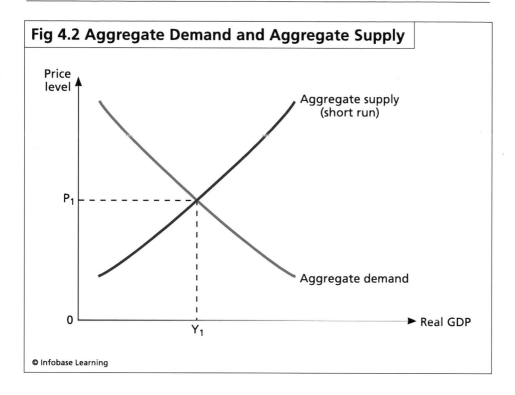

Fig 4.2 Aggregate Demand and Aggregate Supply

Price level — Aggregate supply (short run)

P_1

Aggregate demand

0   Y_1 Real GDP

© Infobase Learning

aggregate supply and the aggregate demand and aggregate supply curves intersect. This occurs at price level P1 and GDP level Y1 in Figure 4.2. However, the economy may not be at the level of GDP that represents full employment. If something happens to cause aggregate demand or aggregate supply to shift, the equilibrium level of prices and GDP will change.

Aggregate demand is the total amount of goods and services that will be purchased at different price levels. It consists of consumption demand by households, investment demand planned by businesses, government demand for goods and services, and the value of exports minus the value of imports. If there are decreases in aggregate demand in the economy, it means that some combination of consumers, businesses, government, and foreigners are now buying fewer U.S. goods and services than in the past. The whole aggregate demand curve would shift to the left. This is shown in panel A of Figure 4.3. An unexpected decrease in aggregate demand may result in unplanned business inventory increases, leading to less production in the future. This in turn leads to a decrease in GDP, a rise in unemployment, and a contraction in the economy. There would be downward pressure on prices. The reverse would be true for increases in aggregate demand, shifting the aggregate demand curve to the right. Businesses would find that their inventories were lower than expected and they would want to increase production in the future. This would lead to an

Fig 4.3 Changes in Aggregate Supply and Aggregate Demand

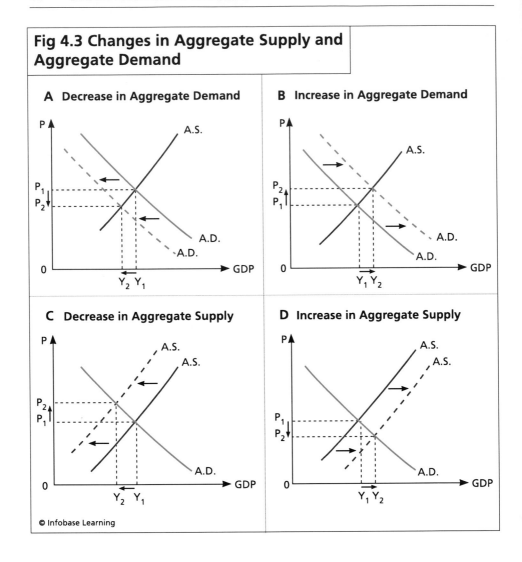

expansion in the economy. An increase in aggregate demand is shown in panel B of Figure 4.3.

Aggregate supply is the total amount of goods and services that will be produced at different price levels. A decrease in aggregate supply in the economy means that producers are producing fewer goods and services than in the past. The whole aggregate supply curve would shift to the left. This is shown in panel C of Figure 4.3. Because fewer goods are produced, GDP falls, unemployment rises, and the economy contracts. A decrease in aggregate supply puts upward pressure on prices. The reverse is true for increases in aggregate supply—the aggregate supply curve shifts to the right. This is shown in panel D. Businesses produce more goods and services, employment likely increases, and the economy expands. An increase in aggregate supply puts downward pressure on prices.

If changes to aggregate demand or aggregate supply are unexpected or sudden, they are referred to as shocks. **Demand shocks** are unexpected, sudden changes in aggregate demand. For example, if there were an unexpected increase in sales taxes, people would have less money to spend after paying these higher taxes and aggregate demand would fall. **Supply shocks** are unexpected, sudden changes in aggregate supply. For example, if oil prices increased unexpectedly (as they did in the 1970s), businesses would have to pay more for fuel and would be able to produce fewer goods and services, leading to a decrease in aggregate supply. Although the examples above are for negative demand and supply shocks, demand and supply shocks can also be positive. Positive shocks occur if events lead to increases in aggregate demand or aggregate supply.

Investment and the Business Cycle

Some of the theories as to why business cycles occur focus on the role of investment, one of the components of aggregate demand. Recall that in macroeconomics, investment means spending by businesses on capital goods. If the economy is expanding, businesses are growing and investment spending increases. Business firms build new factories, buy new machinery, buy new computers, and so on. But at some point, even though business is good, firms will not need to keep expanding. They will have built enough new factories and bought enough new machinery for the time being. This means that the people who had jobs building the factories and the new machinery will no longer have jobs. When workers lose their jobs in the investment industries, their spending falls. This leads to less income for others. Investment theories of the business cycle conclude that such lulls in businesses expansion can move an economy from peak to contraction.

The same reasoning could help explain why an economy comes out of a trough and begins to expand. Even in the Great Depression, when many businesses and banks failed, others remained open. This is explained in part because when capital goods eventually wear out, they need to be replaced. The investment spending to replace capital goods can create jobs for people and help the economy to turn around and begin to expand.

Money Supply and the Business Cycle

Some economists, notably the late Milton Friedman and others called Monetarists, have written that changes in the money supply that affect aggregate demand can cause business cycles. They point to historical evidence that shows that the money supply tends to rise prior to business cycle expansions and tends to decline prior to business cycle contractions. If changes in the money supply cause business cycles, then business cycles could be eliminated if the money supply grew at a steady and predictable rate. The role of the money supply in the economy will be discussed in more detail in Chapter 8.

Expectations

Some economists emphasize that consumers and producers make decisions depending on their expectations for the future. This means that expectations can themselves affect business cycles. If people are forward looking, they react to what they expect to happen and not just what is happening or what has happened. For example, if you are running a business and you expect that your sales will go up in the future, you may decide to hire more workers and increase production now. On a larger scale, such expectations could cause an economy to rise out of a trough and begin to expand. Or if you expected sales to fall in the future, you may cut production and lay off workers in anticipation of the decrease in demand. Widespread expectations such as these could cause the economy to fall from a peak and begin to contract.

Real Business Cycle Theory

Real business cycle theory posits that business cycles are caused by actual events in the economy, and real business cycle theorists believe that real-world phenomena that affect aggregate supply drive changes in business cycles. For example, if there were important improvements in technology or in the quality of resources, supply would go up and the economy would expand. Conversely, if an increase in oil prices made it more expensive to run a business, this would result in a negative supply shock and the economy would contract.

Political Business Cycles

Some people believe that politicians, acting in their own self-interest rather than in the best interest of the public, may at times engage in practices or promote policies that cause business cycles. The theory of political business cycles says that when an election is coming, politicians who hold elective offices have incentives to pass policies that will stimulate the economy and cause an expansion. This will help them to get re-elected. After they are voted into office, they can pass policies that will slow down the economy so that inflation will not become too high. Although there is little evidence to support this theory, elected federal government officials can in fact enact policies that cause the economy to expand and contract.

FORECASTING THE BUSINESS CYCLE

It is often difficult to forecast what will happen in the future with respect to the phases of the business cycle. It is difficult to know, for example, how long an expansion or contraction will last. It is especially difficult to predict the turning points of business cycles—the peaks and troughs. Even the NBER generally announces turning points some months after they have occurred. Despite these difficulties, many people do try to forecast what will happen in the economy in the future. Two common forecasting methods involve using econometric forecasting models and following leading indicators.

Econometric Forecasting Models

Some economists develop models of the economy and then use mathematics and statistics to predict what will happen to the variables in the model such as GDP, employment, and interest rates. **Econometrics** is the field of economics that applies statistics and mathematics to economic models. An econometric model may, for example, hypothesize that GDP depends on a number of variables including consumer spending, business investment, government policies, money supply, and so on. Those working with the model would set up equations and estimate values and weights for those variables, and then get an estimate for GDP. If the model predicts that GDP will increase, it would therefore also predict an expansion. If GDP has been increasing but is predicted to decrease, the model would predict a contraction. Many universities and businesses have their own macroeconomic forecasting models and use them to make predictions about the future direction of the economy.

Leading Indicators

The Conference Board (www.conference-board.org) is an independent non-profit organization that provides research to help businesses and other organizations improve their performance. One thing that the Conference Board does

Conference Board's 10 Leading Economic Indicators

- Average weekly hours, manufacturing
- Average weekly initial claims for unemployment insurance
- Manufacturers' new orders, consumer goods, and materials
- Index of supplier deliveries (vendor performance)
- Manufacturers' new orders, non-defense capital goods
- Building permits, new private housing units
- Stock prices, 500 common stocks
- Money supply, M2
- Interest rate spread, 10-year Treasury bonds less federal funds
- Index of consumer expectations

Source: Conference Board: www.conference-board.org

is provide an index of leading economic indicators designed to predict turning points in the business cycle and how the economy will perform in the future. A **leading indicator** is a measure of economic performance that tends to go up or down before the economy as a whole does so. If the leading indicators are correct, it is possible to predict with some degree of accuracy that economic activity will go up or down in the future.

The Conference Board uses 10 leading indicators to predict what will happen in the U.S. economy (see sidebar). The leading indicators are chosen as likely factors that can signal turning points, or peaks and troughs, in the business cycle. Different indicators in the list are given different weights. The Conference Board combines the weights and values of the 10 indicators and issues a press release once a month reporting its finding for the prior month. For example, on June 17, 2011, the Conference Board announced that its Leading Economic Index increased .8 percent in May 2011, following a decline in April and an increase in March. The indicators that contributed the most to the increase in May 2011 were interest rates, consumer expectations, and new private housing permits (www.conference-board.org/data/bcicountry.cfm?cid=1).

SUMMARY

Although it would be preferable to have the economy grow at a steady and predictable rate without ups and downs leading to inflation and unemployment, the fact is that economies do fluctuate over time. The U.S. economy experienced 33 business cycles between 1854 and 2009, as defined by the National Bureau of Economic Research. Typically, business cycles are characterized by four phases: expansion, peak, contraction or recession, and trough. The cycles (and their phases) vary greatly in terms of length and severity. The aggregate demand / aggregate supply model can be used to investigate causes of business cycles. There are many theories about why business cycles occur. Although business cycles and their turning points are difficult to forecast, econometric models and the Conference Board's Leading Economic Index attempt to do so.

Further Reading

Conference Board. Global Business Cycle Indicators. Retrieved online July 2011 at http://www.conference-board.org/data/bcicountry.cfm?cid=1.

The NBER's Business Cycle Dating Committee. National Bureau of Economic Research. Retrieved online July 2011 at www.nber.org/cycles/recessions.html.

The NBER's Business Cycle Dating Procedure: Frequently Asked Questions. National Bureau of Economic Research. Retrieved online July 2011 at www.nber.org/cycles/recessions_faq.html.

U.S. Business Cycle Expansions and Contractions. National Bureau of Economic Research. Retrieved online July 2011 at www.nber.org/cyclces.html.

CHAPTER 5

PROBLEMS OF THE BUSINESS CYCLE: INFLATION AND UNEMPLOYMENT

Inflation and unemployment are frequently in the news, and both can cause problems for individuals and for the economy as a whole. Rising prices for consumers make it harder for them to afford the things that they want. Rising prices for businesses raise the costs of producing goods. When prices go up throughout the economy, both consumption and production can fall. Unemployment is also bad for the whole economy because fewer goods and services are produced, resulting in fewer goods and services to consume. Not having a job can be devastating for people who are willing and able to work.

We saw in Chapter 4 that inflation and unemployment are problems related to business cycles. Inflation tends to be associated with the peak of the business cycle and unemployment tends to be associated with the trough of the business cycle. However, inflation can occur in downturns and unemployment can be high during expansions or recoveries. It is also possible to have inflation and unemployment occur at the same time. What do we mean by inflation and unemployment, and how are they measured? What are different types of inflation and unemployment? What are the effects of inflation and unemployment on the economy? These are some of the questions that will be addressed in this chapter.

INFLATION
What Is Inflation and How Is It Measured?
Inflation is defined as a sustained increase in the general level of prices. This means that when inflation occurs, prices on average increase. This is different

from when the price of a certain good or service increases. Prices are always changing in a market economy due to supply and demand. For example, if consumers decide that they would like more strawberries and fewer apples, holding everything else constant, the price of strawberries will increase and the price of apples will decrease. But the increase in the price of strawberries does not in itself mean that there is inflation. Inflation occurs when prices are rising throughout the economy. Prices on every good and service may not rise and some prices may even fall. Some prices will rise faster than others. But on average, prices will increase throughout the economy.

The Consumer Price Index

The **Consumer Price Index (CPI)** is the most commonly used measure of inflation in the United States. It is computed monthly by the Bureau of Labor Statistics (www.bls.gov/cpi/). To measure price changes, the BLS looks at the prices of a collection of goods and services that are representative of what a typical urban consumer might buy. The collection of goods and services is sometimes called a "market basket" or a "representative basket." The CPI market basket includes the cost of hundreds of items such as cereal, milk, coffee, chicken, housing, clothing, airline tickets, gasoline, car insurance, prescription drugs, doctors' services, toys, pet products, college tuition, tobacco, and funeral services. The sidebar provides an overview of the major categories of goods and services included in the CPI.

The CPI does not measure price changes for all goods and services in the economy, but only those purchased by typical urban consumers. The BLS decides which goods to include by conducting annual surveys to keep current with consumer buying habits. It collects spending information from families from around the country through surveys and interviews. BLS workers also call or visit stores, offices, doctors' offices, and other establishments each month to learn current prices. To measure price changes from year to year, the BLS

Categories of Goods and Services Included in the CPI

- Food And Beverages
- Housing
- Apparel
- Transportation

- Medical Care
- Recreation
- Education and Communication
- Other Goods and Services

Source: Bureau of Labor Statistics

collects prices on specific goods and services that were available during the prior year. But sometimes a good is no longer available, or the quality has changed over the past year, so it is not exactly the same good. In this case the BLS records the quality change or records the price of the new item. BLS workers who have specialized information about the goods make statistical adjustments for these changes. They try to make sure that the price changes pertain to the same quantity and quality of goods and services over time.

To compare price changes over time, you need to pick a base year or base period to which you can compare current prices. The following formula illustrates how this works:

CPI = Price of market basket in current year (× 100) / price of market basket in base year

For example, if the price of the representative market basket of goods and services was $110 this year and was $100 in the base year we divide 110 by 100 to get 1.1. Traditionally this is multiplied by 100, so in this case, the index is 110. You would interpret this to mean that the prices of goods and services increased by 10 percent over the base year. This means that the rate of inflation since the base year was 10 percent. Or, as indicated by the formula, what cost you $100 in the base year now costs $110. (The formula assumes that adjustments have been made for changes in quality and for changes in the goods in the market basket over time.)

As of 2011, the BLS was using 1982 through 1984 as the official base period. In May 2011, the CPI was 225.964 (www.bls.gov/cpi/cpid1105.pdf). This means that the market basket that cost $100 in 1982–1984 cost $225.96 in 2011. Prices more than doubled between the base period of 1982–1984 and 2011. The inflation rate from 1982–1984 to 2011 was about 126 percent. Note, however, that inflation is most often expressed in terms of year-to-year or month-to-month percentage changes without reference to the official base period.

The Bureau of Labor Statistics actually computes many different price indexes each month. For example, the BLS computes a separate price index that does not include the prices of food and energy, because the prices of these products change frequently. Calculating inflation without including the prices of food and energy yields something that economists call a **core inflation rate**. Figure 5.1 shows annual percentage changes in the CPI-U, the CPI for all urban consumers, from 2001 to 2011. The red line on the graph shows changes in the CPI that include all items, whereas the green line show changes in the core index that excluded food and energy prices. By comparing the red and green lines, you can see that prices of all items change much more when food and energy prices are included, reinforcing the point that food and energy prices are highly volatile. Note as well that both lines are most often above zero, indicating that

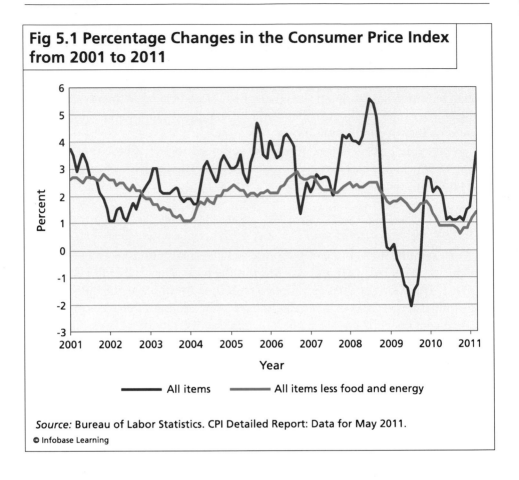

Fig 5.1 Percentage Changes in the Consumer Price Index from 2001 to 2011

All items
All items less food and energy

Source: Bureau of Labor Statistics. CPI Detailed Report: Data for May 2011.
© Infobase Learning

prices have generally risen during the prior 12-month period. For example, for 2011, the CPI increased 3.6 percent over the past 12 months, taking into account food and energy prices.

The CPI is important because it is widely quoted as a measure of how prices are changing. It is also important because some people's wages and salaries are affected by cost of living adjustments called **COLAs** that are tied to the CPI. If you have a COLA tied to the CPI, your income or pension increases when the CPI indicates that inflation has increased. Social Security benefits are subject to COLAs tied to percentage increases in the CPI.

The GDP Price Index

Although the CPI is the measure of inflation that you hear about the most, there are also other measures of inflation. The Bureau of Economic Analysis (BEA: www.bea.gov) computes a GDP price index, which is often referred to as the **Gross Domestic Product Deflator** (GDP Deflator). The **GDP price index**

Certain goods with volatile prices, like food, are not included in the core inflation rate.
(Shutterstock)

includes spending on the goods and services included in GDP, and not just on those goods and services that an urban consumer would buy. It includes prices paid in categories of consumption, investment, government consumption, and net exports. In some cases the GDP price index is a better measure of overall price changes in the economy, but the CPI is a better measure of what is happening to prices of the things that consumers purchase.

The GDP deflator shows the relationship between real GDP and nominal GDP, which were discussed in Chapter 2. It is calculated by the following formula:

$$\text{GDP DEFLATOR} = \text{Nominal GDP } (\times 100) \text{ / real GDP}$$

For example, if nominal GDP for a hypothetical economy was $5 trillion in 2010 and real GDP was $4 trillion, then the GDP deflator would be 125 (5 / 4 = 1.25 x 100 = 125). This means that overall prices have increased by 25 percent since the base year. In a similar manner, the GDP deflator can be used to convert (or "deflate") nominal GDP to real GDP. If we know that nominal GDP is $5 trillion and the GDP deflator is 125, we can divide $5 trillion by 1.25 to get $4 trillion, or real GDP. Today, calculation of the GDP price index takes into account changes in quality and differences in the goods produced over time by linking or "chaining" the base year figures to changes in production in other years.

Table 5.1 shows GDP price deflators for selected years from 1985 through 2010, using 2005 as the base year. Prices of the goods and services in 2005 are weighted to equal 100, so the GDP deflator for 2005 is 100. Prices were lower before 2005, so the price deflators for those years are less than 100. Prices rose after 2005 so the GDP deflators are higher after 2005. For example, in 2010 the GDP price deflator was 110.659, meaning that in 2010 it would have cost $110.66 to buy what cost $100 in 2005. The rate of inflation between 2005 and 2010 was 10.66 percent, or an average of about 2.1 percent per year during that five-year period.

TABLE 5.1
GDP Price Deflators for Selected Years (2005 = base year)

YEAR	GDP Deflator
1985	61.576
1990	72.201
1995	81.536
2000	88.647
2005	100.000
2006	103.257
2007	106.296
2008	108.619
2009	109.615
2010	110.659

Source: Bureau of Economic Analysis National Income and Product Accounts Table 1.1.9

Types of Inflation

Economists sometimes distinguish between two different types of inflation: demand-pull inflation and cost-push inflation. Looking at these two different types of inflation can help identify causes of inflation. The aggregate supply–aggregate demand model introduced in Chapter 4 can be used to explain both types of inflation and why they occur. With demand-pull inflation, an increase in aggregate demand causes prices to rise. With cost-push inflation, a decrease in aggregate supply causes prices to rise.

Demand-pull Inflation

Demand-pull inflation results when people want to buy more goods and services than are available at existing prices. In other words, more goods and services are demanded than supplied at the current price level, and this causes prices to rise. For example, assume that there is one condominium for sale in your neighborhood, and the price listed is $100,000. What if there are four people who would like to buy this condominium, each of whom has enough money to buy it? It is likely that some or all of them will bid up the price above $100,000. The excess demand pulls up the price.

Demand-pull inflation is sometimes defined as "too much money chasing too few goods and services." This means that demand-pull inflation occurs when the amount of money people have to spend goes up more than the goods and services that are available to purchase. This is likely to happen at the peak of the business cycle, when the economy is close to full employment and is producing all that it can. In the long run, increases in the money supply that cause aggregate demand to increase relative to aggregate supply will lead to a sustained increase in prices.

Cost-push Inflation

Cost-push inflation results when business costs increase and businesses pass on their cost increases to consumers in the form of higher prices. Cost-push inflation results from increases in resource costs that affect major parts of the economy. For example, increases in oil prices affect many businesses. It becomes more expensive for businesses to produce and transport their goods and services. To cover their new higher costs, businesses need to raise prices. Economists consider supply shocks from increases in energy costs as the primary reason for inflation in the United States in the 1970s and early 1980s because the increased energy costs pushed up prices for many goods and services.

Increases in the cost of doing business cause aggregate supply to fall and prices to rise in the short run. The decrease in aggregate supply causes unemployment. In the long run, however, if wages and prices are flexible and there is no increase in demand, unemployment eventually leads to decreases in wages and prices. Therefore cost-push inflation, by itself, does not result in sustained inflation in the long run. In reality, it is often difficult to sort out cost-push and demand-pull inflation because changes in costs and demand often occur at the same time.

Effects of Inflation

Economists believe that low rates of inflation (i.e., in the one or two percent range) that are steady and predictable are generally not a problem. But when inflation is high or unexpected, there are several negative effects. Some of these are listed in the sidebar.

Money Loses Value

During inflation, money loses value. For example, if you have $10 to spend on hamburgers and hamburgers cost $1 each, you can buy 10 hamburgers. If inflation occurs and hamburgers now cost $2 each, you will be able to buy only 5 hamburgers. When prices go up, your money loses value because you cannot buy as much as before.

People on Fixed Incomes Are Hurt

Although some people's incomes keep up with inflation through COLAs, others have incomes that are fixed, meaning they remain the same over time. An example of someone with a fixed income is a retired person who has a pension of $2,000 per month and no COLA. Depending on the person's savings and expenses, this might seem like a decent amount of money. But if inflation were 10 percent a year, prices would double about every seven years. A fixed income of $2,000 would not go far in the future.

Difficult to Plan for the Future

If you do not know how fast prices are rising and whether your income will keep up, it is difficult to plan for the future. What if you want to go to graduate school in five years, or you have a baby who will start college in 17 years? How much do

Effects of Inflation

- Money loses value
- People on fixed incomes are hurt
- Difficult to plan for the future
- Lower savings, investment, and growth
- Reduced output and employment (from cost-push inflation)
- Redistribution effect: savers and lenders lose; borrowers gain

you need to save for that future education? These and similar questions confront many individuals during periods of sustained inflation. Business have the same problem. If it is difficult for businesses to plan for the future, there will be less business investment spending. If a business is planning to expand in the future but cannot predict what the cost of expansion will be, the uncertainty decreases the incentive to invest. And less investment leads to lower economic growth in the future.

Lower Savings, Investment, and Growth

During periods of inflation, people have fewer incentives to keep their assets in the form of money or to save money in banks. When people save money in reputable financial institutions, this helps the economy because the money is then available for others to borrow. More savings leads to lower interest rates, which encourages businesses to borrow for investment. However, because money loses value in periods of inflation, people have less incentive to save money. People often buy other assets that they think will hold their value, such as real estate or gold. This causes the price of these assets to increase, further fueling inflation.

Reduced Output and Employment

As discussed earlier, with cost-push inflation, prices rise because aggregate supply declines. The decreases in supply throughout the economy mean that less is produced, so less labor is needed and unemployment rises. Even though this type of inflation may not last indefinitely, the production lost due to cost-push inflation cannot be recovered.

Redistribution of Income

Another problem with inflation is that it can result in an unintended redistribution of income from people who save (or lend) to those who borrow. This occurs if inflation is unexpected, or if the rate of inflation is underestimated. For example, say that I have $100 that I do not need to use and you need $100 for some specific purpose. I agree to lend you $100 for a year, and we do not anticipate any inflation. We may agree that I will charge you 2 percent interest. This 2 percent is the **real rate of interest**—the rate that would exist if there were no inflation.

But what if it turned out that during the year, the country was socked by inflation that averaged 10 percent? You (the borrower) would benefit because the money you borrowed would be worth more (10 percent more) than the money you paid me back. I would be hurt because I would only receive about $90 in purchasing power when you repaid the loan, in exchange for the $100 in purchasing power that I loaned you. Had we both correctly anticipated the inflation, I would have charged you 12 percent interest—the real rate of interest (2 percent) plus the expected rate of inflation (10 percent). This example

The Fisher Effect

Real Interest Rate + Expected Inflation Rate = Market (nominal) Interest Rate

describes the relationship between interest rates and expected inflation rates called the **Fisher Effect**, after American economist Irving Fisher (1867–1947) who first wrote about it. The Fisher Effect predicts that the market or nominal rate of interest will rise with the expected inflation rate. The Fisher Effect, given by the equation in the sidebar, takes place because lenders want to be paid back the same amount of purchasing power that they loaned to others, so they raise interest rates when they expect inflation.

Inflationary Spirals

When people expect inflation to continue, the expectation itself can lead to exactly that effect, and prices spiral upward. For example, assume that inflation exists and you expect it to continue in the future. If you are in the market to buy a house or a car, how does the expectation of inflation affect your buying patterns today? You would want to buy now, before the prices go up. If everyone thinks this way, so that aggregate demand is increasing faster than aggregate supply, this would cause prices to go up. This is why it is sometimes said that inflation "feeds on itself."

Hyperinflation

Hyperinflation occurs when the price level rises very rapidly and there is a very high rate of inflation. Although there is no precise definition of when high inflation becomes hyperinflation, some examples from history help to show what

Worst Hyperinflations of All Time

1. Hungary 1946: Prices doubled every 15.6 hours.
2. Zimbabwe, November 2008: Prices doubled every 24.7 hours.
3. Yugoslavia, January 1994: Prices doubled every 1.4 days.
4. Germany, October 1923: Prices doubled every 3.7 days.
5. Greece, October 1944: Prices doubled every 4.3 days.

Source: www.cnbc.com

hyperinflation is. Perhaps the five worst hyperinflations in history are listed in the sidebar. Following World War I, prices in Germany doubled every three to four days. In Zimbabwe in 2008, prices doubled every 25 hours. And in Hungary in 1946, prices doubled every 16 hours.

Hyperinflations are generally caused by governments printing and circulating excessive amounts of money that are not balanced by economic growth. This causes prices to rise rapidly, and one consequence of this is that money becomes worthless. Although inflation is usually measured as an annual rate of change in prices, with hyperinflation the annual percentage changes are so high that it often makes more sense to talk about how long it takes prices to double. For example, in 2008, the annual inflation rate in Zimbabwe was estimated to be over 11 million percent (www.cnn.com).

What About Deflation?
Our discussion has thus far focused on inflation, or when the average of all prices goes up. But what if prices (on average) fall, as they did during the Great Depression? Deflation occurs when the general level of prices in an economy decreases. To a consumer this may sound like a good thing. But deflation can cause major problems in the economy. For example, if you know that prices are falling, you will postpone purchases until prices are lower. If this happens throughout the economy, the decrease in demand will lead to lower production and higher unemployment. This can cause a deflationary spiral: a downward spiral in prices, production, and employment. It must be noted that inflation has been more of a problem than deflation throughout the world during the 20th and early 21st centuries.

UNEMPLOYMENT
What Is Unemployment and How Is It Measured?
We next turn to unemployment, one of the problems associated with the downward phase of the business cycle. What is the official definition of unemployment? You might logically reason that if someone does not have a job, he or she is unemployed. While it is true that you need a job to be considered employed, everyone who does not have a job is not considered to be officially unemployed. The Bureau of Labor Statistics (www.bls.gov) is the U.S. government agency that determines the official unemployment rate in the United States. To collect information about unemployment, the BLS administers a monthly survey to a sample of the population. This survey is called the Current Population Survey (CPS). To understand how the BLS uses the data gathered to measure unemployment, we need to understand what is meant by *labor force, employed,* and *unemployed.*

The Labor Force

We will begin by dividing the total population of the United States into two groups: those who are in the labor force and those who are not in the labor force. To be a part of the civilian **labor force**, you must be officially employed or unemployed. You also have to be 16 years old or older, not on active duty in the U.S. Armed Forces, and not in an institution such as a prison or a nursing home. If you do not meet these criteria, then you are not in the labor force.

The Employed

You are officially **employed** if you did any work for pay or profit during the reference week of the survey. You are also considered to be employed if you did 15 or more hours of unpaid work in a family business or if you were temporarily absent from a regular job. You do not need to be working full time to be employed. Part-time and temporary workers are also counted as employed. You are also employed if you are out of work because you are sick, on vacation, taking care of a family member, or on strike.

The Unemployed

You are **unemployed** if you are in the labor force and are available for work but do not have a job, and if you have actively looked for a job in the past four weeks. This last point is worth emphasizing: To be officially counted as unemployed, you have to be looking for work while you are not working. Someone who does not have a job but who is not looking for work is not considered part of the labor force and is therefore neither employed nor unemployed. Unemployment is often expressed as a rate or percentage. The **unemployment rate** is found by taking the number of unemployed people and dividing this by the number of people in the labor force:

Unemployment Rate = number of people unemployed / number of people in labor force

Figure 5.2 shows the unemployment rate in the United States from 1990 to 2011. In particular, this figure shows that the unemployment rate ranged from below 4 percent in 2000 to about 10 percent in 2009, following the recession that began in December 2007. Many people argue that the official unemployment rate does not give a complete picture of unemployment for several reasons. One reason is that the unemployment rate ignores **discouraged workers**, that is, those who would like to work but have given up looking for jobs because they do not think there is a chance that they will find anything. Because discouraged workers have dropped out of the labor force and are not actively seeking work, they are not considered to be unemployed. The unemployment rate also does not take into account workers who are said to be underemployed. **Underemployed workers** are people who are working part time but who would like to be

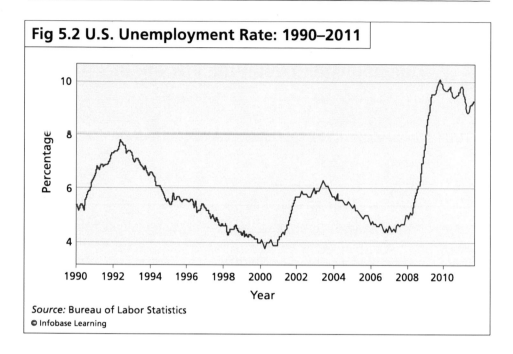

Fig 5.2 U.S. Unemployment Rate: 1990–2011

Percentage / Year

Source: Bureau of Labor Statistics
© Infobase Learning

working full time, or workers who have jobs that do not make the best use of their skills or training. For example, an engineer working at the counter in a fast food restaurant would be considered underemployed.

The BLS computes many statistics about unemployment in addition to the monthly unemployment rate. Some of these are listed in the sidebar on page 72. These additional statistics add detail and provide additional information about the official unemployment rate. The news media will often report employment statistics, the number of new jobs created, and other measures shown in the sidebar.

Types of Unemployment

Economists divide unemployed workers into different categories to provide insights into the causes of unemployment and what can be done to decrease unemployment. Different types of unemployment require different remedies. The major types of unemployment are frictional, structural, and cyclical.

Frictional Unemployment

Frictional unemployment occurs when workers are between jobs (e.g., when they voluntarily quit one job to look for another job) or when they look for their first job. This type of unemployment is sometimes called "search unemployment" because people are searching for a new job or a better job. Generally speaking there are enough job openings available for the frictionally

Some Figures Related to Unemployment Computed by the BLS

- Unemployment rate
- Average hourly earnings
- Changes in the number of non-farm payroll jobs
- Number of employed people
- Employment rate
- Unemployment by groups such as age, sex, and race
- Number of people unemployed for less than 5 weeks and more than 27 weeks
- Labor force participation rate
- Number of involuntary part-time workers
- Employment in different types of jobs, such as manufacturing and government
- Length of average work week
- State, local, and international unemployment rates
- Layoff statistics

Source: Bureau of Labor Statistics

unemployed, but it takes time for a worker in this group to find an appropriate job. Much frictional unemployment is voluntary. In a free market economy, we do not want to totally eliminate frictional unemployment because this would take away people's freedom to search for new jobs. Nonetheless, frictional unemployment can be decreased by providing better information to job seekers and those hiring workers. Having better information would shorten the length of the search time.

Some people argue that unemployment compensation increases frictional unemployment. This may be true for some people because unemployment compensation pays people when they are not working, so they may not be in much of a hurry to find a job. But not all unemployed people qualify for unemployment compensation. To receive unemployment benefits from the government, you have to have worked for a considerable amount of time in a prior job, and you have to have lost your prior job for an acceptable reason. If you quit your job or were fired for poor performance, you would not qualify. Rules about unemployment compensation are set by individual states.

Structural Unemployment

Structural unemployment occurs when unemployed workers do not have the skills for the jobs that are available. In other words, there are job openings, but the structurally unemployed do not qualify for those jobs. For example, an older person who has never learned to use computers would not qualify for any job requiring computer skills, even if many jobs in this field were available. By the same token, a high school dropout would be disqualified from many jobs because he or she lacks the education required for those jobs. Because there are always mismatches between available jobs and the skills of job seekers, some structural unemployment will always exist. Nonetheless, structural unemployment can be decreased through education and job training programs.

Cyclical Unemployment

Cyclical unemployment occurs because of the business cycle. When the economy is declining and in a contraction, cyclical unemployment increases. In a contraction, GDP falls and the decrease in production causes some workers to lose their jobs. When the economy is expanding and GDP is increasing, cyclical unemployment falls. Reducing cyclical unemployment requires dealing with the business cycle. How the government and central bank can try to reduce cyclical unemployment will be discussed in chapters 6 and 8.

Figure 5.3 shows how unemployment changes during business cycles. The shaded bars in this figure show recessions that occurred between 1969 and 2008. During each recession, the pattern shows rising unemployment. And in the following expansions, unemployment was generally falling. There are of course, some increases in unemployment during some expansions, for example in the expansions of 1976–1977 and 2003–2004. But overall, the unemployment rate changes are fairly consistent within the business cycle, increasing during recessions and decreasing during expansions.

Because some frictional and structural unemployment will always exist, the target rate for unemployment is not zero. The **natural rate of unemployment** is the rate that would exist if there were only frictional and structural unemployment, but no cyclical unemployment. It is sometimes also said that full employment exists when unemployment is equal to the natural rate. But note that in this context, full employment does not mean that there is zero unemployment. The natural rate of unemployment is currently estimated to be around five percent. The BLS reported that unemployment was 9.2 percent in June 2011, and this means that cyclical unemployment was over 4 percent.

You may have also heard the term seasonal unemployment. **Seasonal unemployment** occurs due to seasonal or recurring changes in available jobs or in the labor supply. For example, seasonal unemployment increases during summer months as more students enter the labor force and look for jobs. In

Fig 5.3 U.S. Unemployment Rate for Persons 16 and Older, Seasonally Adjusted, Quarterly Averages, 1969–2008

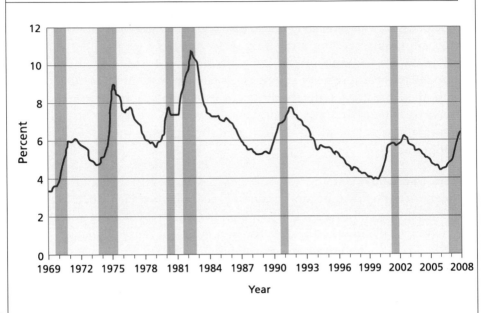

Note: Shaded areas represent recessions as designated by the National Bureau of Economic Research (NBER).

Source: Bureau of Labor Statistics, Current Population Survey.

© Infobase Learning

some areas, it increases in winter months because farm workers are out of work due to the weather. The BLS addresses these seasonal changes in unemployment by reporting seasonal adjustments in monthly unemployment rates.

Effects of Unemployment
Personal Costs

On a personal level, the effects of unemployment vary. But all unemployed individuals have one thing in common—the loss of income that would have been earned had they been working. Because that income was not earned, all of these people were subject (albeit to varying degrees) to decreased consumption and lifestyle changes. For those supporting family members, the loss of potential income also affects spouses and children. It can also means dipping into savings, relying on loans or donations from others, or relying on government unemployment programs to get by. When these sources dry up, there may be few options beyond applying for government welfare programs for those who qualify.

People who are unemployed often lose self-esteem because they are unable to find work, and lack of self-confidence may make it harder to find a job. Unemployment can also cause other problems for individuals and families, including increased divorce rates and health problems resulting from increased stress. And there are problems for society at large, discussed below.

Of course, everyone who is unemployed does not end up getting divorced, or ending up on welfare. For people who are unemployed only for a short time, for those whose job before unemployment was part-time, and/or for those with an employed spouse, the future is seldom so bleak. Moreover, people who have been unemployed for a short time are more likely to find jobs than those who have been unemployed for a long time, an additional factor compounding the problems of long-term unemployment.

Problems for the Economy

In addition to the personal costs of unemployment, there are consequences for the economy as a whole. For example, when unemployment rates go up, crime rates go up. And when workers are unemployed today, they are not producing goods and services today. This lost production cannot be recovered—it is lost forever. When unemployment is above the natural rate, GDP is lower than its potential. By some estimates, for every one percent increase in unemployment above the natural rate, GDP will decrease by two percent below its potential. This relationship is called **Okun's Law** (or Okun's rule of thumb) after Arthur Okun, the economist who first delineated the relationship.

SUMMARY

Inflation and unemployment can cause problems, both for individuals and for the economy. When the average of all prices rises, money loses value and it is hard to plan for the future. Inflation leads to decreases in savings and investment, which in turn leads to decreased economic growth. In extreme cases of hyperinflation, money becomes worthless and the monetary system must be restructured. Classifying types of inflation as demand-pull or cost-push helps identify underlying causes of inflation in the long run and in the short run. Unemployment often has serious consequences for individuals and families. For the economy, unemployment results in lost output and less production than is potentially possible. Frictional, structural, and cyclical unemployment have different underlying causes that call for different potential solutions.

Further Reading

Borbely, James M. U.S. Labor Market in 2008: Economy in Recession. Bureau of Labor Statistics. Retrieved online July 2011 at http://www.bls.gov/opub/mlr/2009/03/art1full.pdf.

Bureau of Economic Analysis: Gross Domestic Product (GD) Price Index. Retrieved online July 2011 and www.bea.gov/glossary/.

Bureau of Economic Analysis Table 1.1.9 Implicit Price Deflators for Gross Domestic Product. Retrieved online July 2011 at http://www.bea.gov/national/nipaweb/.

Consumer Price Index. Bureau of Labor Statistics. Retrieved online July 2100 at http://www.bls.gov/cpi/.

Crawford, Malik, and Jonathan Church, editors. CPI Detailed Report: Data for May 2011. Bureau of Labor Statistics. Retrieved online July 2011 at http://www.bls.gov/cpi/cpid1105.pdf.

Toscano, Paul. The Worst Hyperinflation Situations of All Time. Retrieved online July 2011 at http://www.cnbc.com/id/41532451/The_Worst_Hyperinflation_Situations_of_All_Time?

Unemployment Rate. Bureau of Labor Statistics Data. Retrieved online July 2011 at http://data.bls.gov/pdq/SurveyOutputServlet.

"Zimbabwe Inflation Hits 11,200,000 Percent." August 19, 2008. CNN.com: retrieved online July 2011 at http://edition.cnn.com/2008/BUSINESS/08/19/zimbabwe.inflation/index.html.

CHAPTER 6

FISCAL POLICY AND THE NATIONAL DEBT

Because the government controls taxes and decides how much it will spend, it can use fiscal policy to try to improve things in the economy. **Fiscal policy** is defined as changes in government spending or taxes to try to stabilize the economy. Government works to **stabilize** the economy by attempting to smooth out the problems of inflation and unemployment associated with the peak and trough of the business cycle. Fiscal policy also tries to keep GDP growing at its potential rate and to keep actual GDP close to potential GDP. **Potential GDP** is the level that would exist if there were full employment in the economy.

Fiscal policy is controversial and the subject of many political debates. Part of the controversy centers on whether the government should take an active or passive role with fiscal policy, something which will be discussed in Chapter 9. Part of the controversy centers on beliefs about the appropriate level of taxation. And part of the controversy centers on the effects of fiscal policy on the national debt. In this chapter we will look at the basics of fiscal policy. We will also look at the issue of the national debt and some of the perceived and real problems that it has on the economy.

THE TOOLS OF FISCAL POLICY

The word fiscal originated during the Roman Empire, when the word "fisc" referred to the government's treasury. (Note that fiscal is not the same as physical, which refers to the body or nature.) Fiscal policy refers to the government treasury because changing taxes and government spending are its two main tools. Taxes bring revenue into the government treasury, while government spending takes money out.

Traditional fiscal policy works by influencing aggregate demand, although we will discuss supply-side fiscal policy as well. Recall that aggregate demand consists of household demand for consumption goods, business planned demand for investment goods, government demand for goods and services, and the demand for exports minus the demand for imports. Business demand for investment goods does not include unplanned changes to inventories that take place when businesses do not sell everything they had hoped to sell. The formula for aggregate demand is shown below.

$$\text{AGGREGATE DEMAND} = C + I_{pl} + G + (X\text{-}M)$$
$$C = \text{consumption spending}$$
$$I_{pl} = \text{planned investment spending}$$
$$G = \text{government purchases}$$
$$X\text{-}M = \text{exports (X) - imports (M)}$$

Taxes
Effect on Aggregate Demand
Taxes affect aggregate demand because they affect how much income households and businesses have to spend on goods and services. When the government decreases taxes, households and businesses have more after-tax income to spend. This increases aggregate demand, holding everything else constant.

TABLE 6.1
Major Sources of Government Revenue (Fiscal Year 2011)

Individual Income Taxes	$ 1.1 trillion
Corporate Income Taxes	$ 181 billion
Social Security and Other Payroll Taxes	$ 819 billion
Excise Taxes	$ 72 billion
Estate and Gift Taxes	$ 7.4 billion
Customs Duties	$ 29.5 billion
Other receipts	$ 102.8 billion
Total Receipts	**$ 2.3 trillion**

Source: Office of Management and Budget: www.whitehouse.gov

If the economy is experiencing unemployment and GDP is below its potential level, the increase in aggregate demand can lead to more production, more jobs, and an increase in GDP and employment. When the government raises taxes, households and businesses have less after-tax income to spend. This decreases aggregate demand, holding everything else constant. If the economy is near full employment, a decline in demand can take pressure off rising prices and inflation.

Major Sources of Federal Government Tax Revenue

The major sources of federal government tax revenue are shown in Table 6.1 and in Figure 6.1. The three major sources today are individual income taxes, payroll taxes, and corporate income taxes. In 2011, individual income tax receipts accounted for about 48 percent of government revenue, payroll taxes about 36 percent, and corporate income taxes about 8 percent (www.whitehouse.gov). A **payroll tax** is the tax that an employer is required to withhold from your paycheck. Examples of payroll taxes are withholdings for Social Security and Medicare. Other taxes include excise taxes, estate and gift taxes, and customs duties. **Excise taxes** are taxes on the sale or consumption of goods, such as gasoline or tobacco. Excise taxes have decreased as a source of revenue since the 1930s,

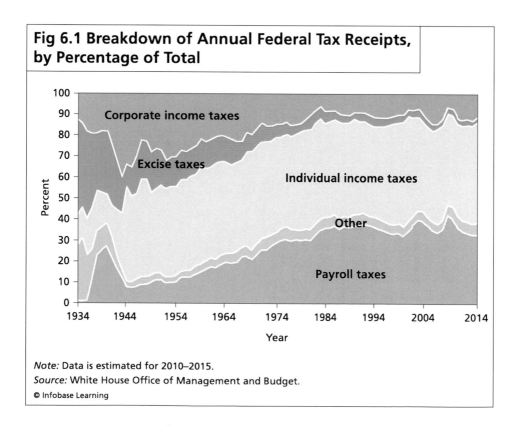

Fig 6.1 Breakdown of Annual Federal Tax Receipts, by Percentage of Total

Note: Data is estimated for 2010–2015.
Source: White House Office of Management and Budget.
© Infobase Learning

whereas individual income taxes and payroll tax receipts have increased as a percentage of the total taxes collected.

Government Spending
Effect on Aggregate Demand

Government spending on goods and services is one of the components of aggregate demand. When the government spends on the military or roads, for example, this can increase employment and production. When the government pays to build a bridge, people are employed to build the bridge and then have more income to spend. When government spending decreases, less is spent on goods and services. Decreases in government spending will decrease aggregate demand, if nothing else changes. If inflation is a problem, the decrease in demand can take pressure off rising prices and help to lower inflation.

Major Categories of Government Spending

The major categories of government spending are shown in Figure 6.2. The graph shows government spending in four categories as a percentage of total government spending beginning in 1962 and projected through 2012. The largest category is mandatory spending on programs such as Social Security, Medicaid, and Medicare. Because current laws entitle people with certain

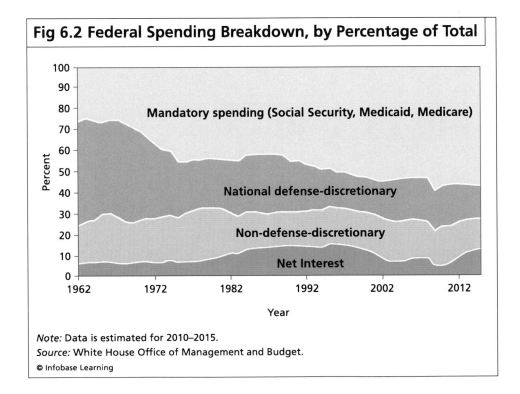

Fig 6.2 Federal Spending Breakdown, by Percentage of Total

Note: Data is estimated for 2010–2015.
Source: White House Office of Management and Budget.
© Infobase Learning

characteristics to receive funding from these programs, the government would have to change the laws to cut spending in these areas. The amount spent on these programs each year depends on how many people qualify for them. In 2011, the funds allocated for these programs represented over 56 percent of federal government spending. The second largest government spending category is discretionary spending on national defense, which represented about 19.4 percent of total government spending in 2011. Discretionary spending on programs not related to national defense, such as spending on education and infrastructure, represented about 17.5 percent of the total. Interest on the national debt accounted for about 6.5 percent of total government spending in 2011 (www. WashingtonPost.com).

The discretionary categories of government spending make up about 37 percent of the total amount, a little over one third. The mandatory portions of the government budget, spending on the interest on the national debt and for entitlement programs such as Social Security, make up over two-thirds of total government spending. These mandatory portions of the budget limit the flexibility of the government to cut its spending, because it cannot cut the mandatory programs without changing the laws. Those who do not believe that defense spending should be cut impose even greater limits on spending flexibility.

EXPANSIONARY AND CONTRACTIONARY FISCAL POLICY
Expansionary Fiscal Policy
The government engages in **expansionary fiscal policy** when it increases spending or decreases taxes in order to increase aggregate demand, production, and employment. Expansionary fiscal policy is used to address recessions or other periods of high unemployment and sluggish economic growth. Figure 6.3 shows the intent of expansionary fiscal policy using the aggregate supply–aggregate demand model.

The price level for the economy is on the vertical axis, and output or GDP is on the horizontal axis. Note that when GDP increases, employment generally increases as well because more workers are needed to produce more output. The aggregate supply curve is drawn as a horizontal line at the lower levels of GDP because when high unemployment exists (a short-run situation), businesses can increase their production without raising their prices. High unemployment is the problem that expansionary fiscal policy wishes to address.

In Figure 6.3, the economy begins at equilibrium point 1 with aggregate demand at level AD1 and GDP at level Q1. The full employment level of GDP is much higher than Q1, so the economy is experiencing unemployment. Currently there is not enough demand to purchase the output that would be produced at full employment. If the government were to increase its spending, aggregate demand could increase through increases in G (government spending). If it were to lower taxes, aggregate demand could increase through increases in

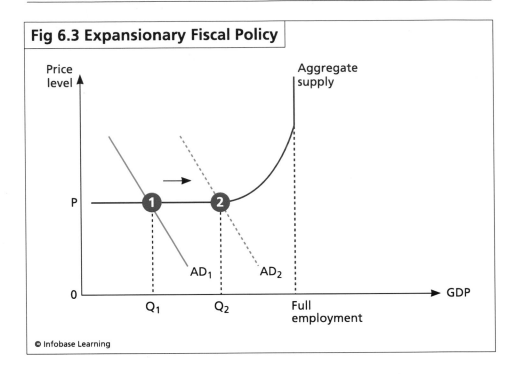

Fig 6.3 Expansionary Fiscal Policy

C (consumption) or I (investment). The aggregate demand curve would shift to the right and could eventually reach a level such as AD2. The economy would move to equilibrium point Q2. Both output and employment have increased. Further increases in aggregate demand could bring the economy to the full employment level of GDP.

Contractionary Fiscal Policy

Contractionary fiscal policy takes place when the government decreases its spending or increases taxes in order to decrease aggregate demand. Contractionary fiscal policy is designed to address inflation or potential inflation. Figure 6.4 shows an aggregate supply–aggregate demand approach to contractionary fiscal policy. Inflation tends to be a problem at the peak of the business cycle when the economy is at or near full employment. Therefore the aggregate supply curve is drawn as a vertical line at the full employment level of GDP. The aggregate supply curve becomes vertical at full employment (the long-run situation) because sustainable increases in production cannot take place with the current level of resources, regardless of the price level.

In Figure 6.4, the economy begins at equilibrium point 1, where the price level is P1 and GDP is at its full employment level. If the government wanted to decrease the price level, it could lower aggregate demand by decreasing its spending or by raising taxes. If aggregate demand fell from AD1 to AD2, the economy would eventually reach the new equilibrium at point 2. Prices would fall from P1 to P2, and in the long run, the economy would again achieve the full employment level of GDP. Before wages and prices adjust to the new equilibrium level at P2, the decrease in aggregate demand could cause temporary unemployment at price level P1. Whether prices adjust quickly or are "sticky" and adjust slowly is a matter of debate. But the intent of contractionary fiscal policy is to cause the price level to fall without decreasing long-run output and employment. This is shown in the figure by the movement from equilibrium point 1 to equilibrium point 2.

Examples of Fiscal Policy

A recent example of expansionary fiscal policy is the American Recovery and Reinvestment Act, a $787 billion stimulus package passed by Congress in February 2009 during the Obama administration. It included both tax decreases and government spending increases. The tax decreases accounted for 27 percent to 35 percent of the total, depending on how the tax measures are categorized. The government spending increases included direct spending on things like unemployment benefits and food stamps, and appropriations spending for infrastructure and science (http://cnnmoney.com).

An example of contractionary fiscal policy to address inflation occurred in 1982, when Congress reversed some of the tax decreases that were enacted in 1981. Congress was concerned that the 1981 tax decreases would cause inflation

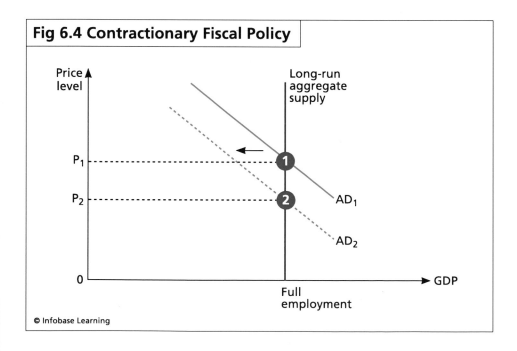

Fig 6.4 Contractionary Fiscal Policy

© Infobase Learning

to rise. Another example of contractionary fiscal policy occurred in 1968, when President Johnson proposed a tax surcharge because of concerns about inflation stemming from increased spending for the Vietnam War. The tax surcharge was essentially a one-time tax increase.

AUTOMATIC FISCAL POLICY

The examples of fiscal policy described above are examples of discretionary fiscal policy. **Discretionary fiscal policy** takes place when the government deliberately decides to change taxes or spending to deal with a certain situation, such as a recession or inflation. However, some fiscal policy takes place automatically. **Automatic stabilizers** are changes in taxes and government spending that take place because of already existing legislation. Automatic stabilizers are also called built-in stabilizers and non-discretionary fiscal policy. They are non-discretionary countercyclical tools because they automatically deal with the problems of the business cycle. The government does not have to pass new legislation to put them into effect.

Income Taxes

Recall that when the business cycle is near its peak and inflation may be a problem, a proactive countermeasure is to constrain aggregate demand. With respect to fiscal policy, this would involve increasing taxes and decreasing government spending. The United States has a progressive income tax system, which means that people with higher incomes pay higher marginal tax rates. The **marginal tax rate** is the rate paid on the last dollar of taxable income earned. For example, between 2010 and 2012, income tax rates ranged from 10 percent for a single person earning income of $8,375 or less, up to 35 percent on the income earned over $373,650. There were six income tax brackets in all.

At the peak of the business cycle, more people are employed and have higher incomes. Therefore they automatically fall into higher tax brackets and pay more income taxes. This is what we want to have happen with fiscal policy during inflation. When there is high unemployment, tax receipts fall because fewer people are working and incomes fall. People end up in lower tax brackets, which decreases the amount of taxes that they pay. Decreasing taxes during recessions is what we want to have happen for fiscal policy to address high unemployment.

Unemployment Insurance

Unemployment insurance is another example of an automatic stabilizer. Through the U.S. Department of Labor, the federal government provides benefits to eligible workers who become unemployed for reasons that are not their fault, and who meet other requirements. At the peak of the business cycle, fewer people are unemployed, so government spending for unemployment compensation falls. This helps to take pressure off rising prices. When unemployment becomes a problem, government spending on unemployment compensation increases. This helps to increase aggregate demand. Thus, government spending is decreased during inflation and increased during recessions automatically, which are the desired effects of countercyclical fiscal policy.

THE MULTIPLIER PROCESS

If the current level of GDP in a country were $8 trillion, and the full-employment target level of GDP were $10 trillion, would the government have to increase spending or decrease taxes by $2 trillion to close the GDP gap? According to the multiplier theory, the answer to this question is no. Economists use the term **multiplier** to mean a change in an economic variable that brings about greater changes in another variable. The expenditure multiplier is the idea that any change in spending can have a greater effect on output (GDP) and income. Although there are several economic multipliers, the term multiplier in this discussion concerns the expenditure multiplier.

Here is an example of how the expenditure multiplier might work. Suppose that after being unemployed, you are hired by the government for a job to help build a bridge, and your income is $40,000 a year, after taxes. What will you do with your $40,000? You will probably spend a good deal of this money, but you may also save some. (In this context, your savings includes personal investment such as buying stock or bonds.) Say that you decided to spend $36,000 of your income over the course of the year, and you decided to save the other $4,000. The $36,000 then becomes income to someone else. For example, if you bought new furniture with some of your income, the furniture seller would then have more income to spend. If you spent some of your income on vegetables at your local farmers' market, the vegetable farmer would have more income to spend. This multiplier process would continue as the furniture seller and the farmer spent some of their new income. The theory behind the multiplier effect is that whenever someone spends, someone else gets income and will also spend.

John Maynard Keynes (1883–1946), a British economist and the originator of many ideas behind macroeconomics today, was an early proponent of using expansionary fiscal policy to address the lack of aggregate demand during the Great Depression. Keynes used the term **marginal propensity to consume** (MPC) to describe the percentage of a change in income that is consumed. The **marginal propensity to save** (MPS) is the percentage of a change in income that is saved. In our example, you spent 90 percent of your income and saved 10 percent. Thus, your MPC is .9 (or 90 percent), and your MPS is .1 (or ten percent). Table 6.1 shows a hypothetical example for the multiplier effect, assuming that everyone's MPC is .9.

Table 6.1 shows the first five rounds of this multiplier process, as well as the total of all of the rounds (including those not shown). Based on an initial

TABLE 6.1
The Multiplier Effect (MPC = .9)

Expenditure Round	Change in Income	Change in Consumption	Change in Savings
1.	$40,000	$36,000.00	$4,000.00
2.	$36,000	$32,400.00	$3,600.00
3.	$32,400	$29,160.00	$3,240.00
4.	$29,160	$26,244.00	$2,916.00
5.	$26,244	$23619.60	$2,624.40
(Multiplier process continues)			
Total of all changes	**$400,000**	**$360,000.00**	**$40,000.00**

increase in government spending of $40,000 and an MPC of .9 for the economy, total income can increase by as much as $400,000. In this example, the multiplier is 10 ($40,000 x 10 = $400,000). The formula to find the multiplier based on the MPC and the MPS is

Expenditure multiplier = 1 / MPS = 1 / 1-MPC

This formula shows that if the MPC were to fall, the multiplier would also fall. For example, if the MPC were .75, the multiplier would be 4 (1/.25). If the MPC were .5, the multiplier would be 2 (1/.5).

The multiplier effect is usually seen to work through changes in aggregate demand. Multiplier effects can take place from changes in consumption, investment, and net exports as well as from changes in government spending. Note that the multiplier can also work in reverse. For example, if the government decreased spending on building bridges and you lost your $40,000-a-year job (and did not find another one), you would spend and save less. Your decreased spending would result in others having less to spend, and so on.

Although our example gives a basic explanation of the multiplier, real-world application of the multiplier effect is more complex. For one thing, other things are factored into the equation in addition to the MPC. Moreover, according to Harvard economist Robert Barro and others, there are different multiplier effects for different types of spending, such as defense spending and non-defense spending. There is also evidence that the multiplier effect varies with the level of unemployment, and that the effect is greater for tax decreases than for government spending increases. Another consideration is evidence that government spending may cause private investment spending to decrease, so the value of the multiplier is much lower than the formula predicts. If this occurs, the government stimulus packages may not have their intended multiplier effects.

SUPPLY-SIDE FISCAL POLICY

The theory behind traditional fiscal policy is that it will increase aggregate demand and then lead to increased output. **Supply-side fiscal policy** focuses on measures that will increase production and therefore increase aggregate supply. Supply-side fiscal policy is also called supply-side economics. It focuses on reducing marginal tax rates to provide incentives to workers and businesses. From the supply-side perspective, the rationale for lowering taxes is that if workers have lower marginal tax rates, they will have incentives to work more, which will in turn increase output. If businesses pay lower marginal tax rates, they will have incentives to invest more, which will increase output. Supply-side economics is often associated with the presidency of Ronald Reagan. Supply-side theories will also be discussed in Chapter 9.

PROBLEMS WITH CONDUCTING FISCAL POLICY

The discussion about the multiplier included the observation that the actual multiplier in practice is much lower than would be predicted by the simple multiplier formula, and this limits the effectiveness of fiscal policy. But there are additional factors that also limit fiscal policy's power to achieve desired outcomes. Some of these problems relate to timing and lags and a phenomenon called crowding out. Others relate to political preferences for expansionary versus contractionary fiscal policy. Because of these problems, some economists recommend that fiscal policy be conducted by following rules that focus on long-run goals rather than on the discretion of policy makers.

Timing Problems

Fiscal policy is subject to different types of time lags that can reduce its effectiveness. A **recognition lag** is the length of time between when a problem occurs and when policy makers realize that it has occurred. Because economic forecasting is imprecise and there are many different things occurring in the economy at one time, it is not always easy to recognize inflation or a recession as soon as they begin. There is also a **decision lag**, which is the amount of time it takes for policy makers to agree on what to do about a problem. With fiscal policy, the decision lag can be lengthy because politicians have different opinions, making the political process of passing new legislation lengthy. It can also take time to implement a fiscal policy measure. There is an also an **effect lag**, the amount of time it takes for a policy to affect output, employment, or prices in the economy. For example, if the government implemented a policy to lower tax rates to address the problem of unemployment, it could take time for taxpayers to increase their spending in response to the lower rates. This would delay the effects on aggregate demand and aggregate supply, and on output and employment.

Crowding Out

Another problem affecting the effectiveness of fiscal policy is called crowding out. **Crowding out** occurs when increases in government spending financed through borrowing result in increases in interest rates and a decline in private spending. The government borrows in the same financial markets as private borrowers, so government borrowing increases the demand for funds available for borrowing. This causes interest rates, the cost of borrowing, to rise. Crowding out occurs because the increased interest rates lead to less borrowing for private investment spending and private consumption. Thus, government spending simply replaces or crowds out the private spending. As a result, the government sector of the economy becomes larger and the private sector smaller. Crowding out from government borrowing may be a reason why multiplier effects from government stimulus efforts are not as significant as we would expect them to be. The extent to which crowding out occurs is a matter of debate.

Political Preferences for Expansionary Policy

Historically, fiscal policies addressing unemployment have often been more politically popular than those addressing inflation. For example, imagine that you were a member of Congress and were hoping to get reelected. Your constituents may be happier if you supported lower taxes and more spending on projects in your local area than if you supported higher taxes and less local spending. Some people believe, therefore, that traditional demand-side fiscal policy is biased toward expansionary policies rather than contractionary policies. This bias may become less prevalent as more people become concerned about government borrowing and the national debt.

THE NATIONAL DEBT
The Debt and Deficits

The government has a budget for every fiscal year. In the United States, the **fiscal year** runs from October 1 through September 30. In any given fiscal year, if government revenues are equal to government expenditures, the government has a **balanced budget**. If the government takes in more revenue than it spends in a given year, it has a **budget surplus**. If the government spends more than the revenue it receives in a given year, it has a **budget deficit**. The **national debt** is

Balanced Budgets, Surpluses, and Deficits

G = Government spending
T = Tax and other revenues
If G = T, the result is Balanced Budget
If T > G, the result is Budget Surplus
If G > T, the result is Budget Deficit

the total of all of the annual deficits, minus any surpluses, of the federal government over time. The debt of the federal government goes by a variety of names, including the national debt, the public debt, the federal government debt, and the U.S. government debt.

Because the U.S. government has had many more deficit years than surplus years and higher overall deficits than surpluses, the country has a hefty national debt today. You may find out the exact amount of the national debt by visiting the U.S. Treasury Department Web site: www.publicdebt.treas.gov. The sidebar below shows that in September 2011 the national debt was about $14.7 trillion, whereas the annual deficit was estimated to be $1.3 trillion. This was expected to be the third largest deficit in the past 65 years.

Budget deficits arise from two sources. One of these sources is discretionary fiscal policy, specifically when the government decides to increase spending and lower taxes to address problems in the economy. Deficits occurring from discretionary fiscal policy are called **structural deficits**. But government budget deficits also result from the business cycle, because when the economy contracts, tax revenues fall and government spending goes up to accommodate legally mandated automatic stabilizers. Deficits occurring because of the business cycle are called **cyclical deficits**. Because of the possibility of cyclical deficits, you cannot always look at the existence or size of

The Debt versus the Deficit

U.S. National Debt as of September 15, 2011: $14,696,963,569,782.73
Source: U.S. Treasury Department

Projected federal Budget Deficit for 2011: $1,300,000,000,000
Source: Congressional Budget Office

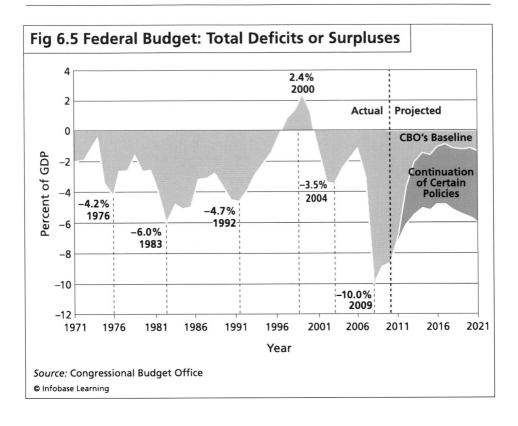

Fig 6.5 Federal Budget: Total Deficits or Surpluses

Source: Congressional Budget Office

© Infobase Learning

a budget deficit and assume that the government is engaging in expansionary fiscal policy.

Figure 6.5 shows the total budget deficits and surpluses for the 40-year period from 1971 through 2011, as reported by the Congressional Budget Office. The deficits and surpluses are reported as a percentage of GDP. Projected deficits from 2011 through 2021 are also shown, but these projections depend on whether or not certain polices continue. We see that deficits have occurred in most years, with surpluses occurring during the Clinton administration from 1998 to 2000 and into 2001. The 2009 and 2010 deficits were higher as a percentage of GDP than in past years, reaching 10 percent in 2009 and close to nine percent in 2010. These are the highest deficits as a percentage of GDP since World War II. In 1942 deficits reached 14 percent of GDP and then jumped to 30 percent in 1943. Deficits as a percentage of GDP then fell to 23 percent in 1944 and to 22 percent in 1945. The deficit situation changed soon after World War II ended, and there were surpluses from 1947 though 1949 (*Economic Report of the President*).

How Is the Debt Financed?
Where does the government get the money to run a deficit? The answer to this question is that the government borrows money from others by selling bonds.

A **bond** is a financial instrument representing debt to the issuer, so it can be viewed as an IOU. If the government sells bonds, it is borrowing money. If you buy a government bond, you are lending the government money. Bonds pay interest, and U.S. government bonds are a very safe investment, so many people are willing to buy them. The total amount of the national debt is represented by the total value of government bonds outstanding.

Who Owns the U.S. Government Debt?

The chart in Figure 6.6 shows who owns the bonds that make up the national debt. About 42 percent of the debt is held by intergovernmental agencies such as Social Security, Medicare, and other government programs. This also includes the bonds held by the Federal Reserve System, the U.S. central bank. The other 58 percent is the publicly held debt, which includes the amount held by foreign individuals and governments (31 percent) and by domestic private investors in the United States (27 percent; *Treasury Bulletin* 9/2011). Domestic private investors include private individuals, banks, state and local governments, insurance companies, and mutual funds. Note that over two-thirds (69 percent) of the debt is held by Americans, and less than one-third (31 percent) is held by foreigners. So the government owes most of this money to U.S. citizens and businesses and to itself. This means that

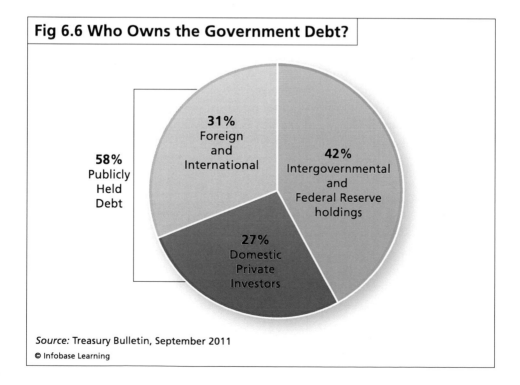

Fig 6.6 Who Owns the Government Debt?

31% Foreign and International

42% Intergovernmental and Federal Reserve holdings

58% Publicly Held Debt

27% Domestic Private Investors

Source: Treasury Bulletin, September 2011

© Infobase Learning

American taxpayers owe money to American bondholders. Many taxpayers are also bondholders.

However, the foreign-held portion of the debt has been growing over time. Today, over half of the publicly held debt is held by foreigners. In 2000, foreign ownership of publicly held debt was only about 36 percent. According to the U.S Government Accounting Office, the foreign countries or regions holding the greatest number of U.S. government bonds (ranked from highest to lowest) are China, Japan, Middle East oil exporting countries, Russia, Taiwan, and Hong Kong.

U.S. government bonds are attractive to foreign investors for their security, for possible favorable returns, and because the U.S. dollar is the major reserve currency in the world today. A **reserve currency** is a foreign currency held by financial institutions and central banks that can be used to pay off international debts. Because U.S. government bonds can be sold for U.S. dollars, they serve as a source of dollars in foreign countries.

What Are the Problems Associated with the National Debt?

The problems associated with the debt are often referred to as the "burden of the debt." What are the individual components of this burden and who really bears the burden? And which factors seem to be a problem related to the national debt but are not?

Bankruptcy

Bankruptcy occurs when someone who has borrowed money cannot pay it back. One potential problem that some people cite about the national debt is that because the government owes a great deal of money, it must be going bankrupt. However, as long as the government can continue to sell bonds, it can continue to refinance or roll over the debt. For example, if you own $10,000 in government bonds that come due this year, the government will pay you back your $10,000. This would decrease the debt by $10,000. But if the government wants another $10,000, it can sell $10,000 bond in new bonds. As long as there are willing buyers for government bonds, bankruptcy is not a problem.

Are These Problems from the National Debt?

- Government bankruptcy
- Interest on the debt
- Burden on future generations
- Foreign-held debt
- Inflation
- Crowding out

Interest on the Debt

Just because the government is not going bankrupt does not mean that we want the debt to go on forever. We saw earlier that over six percent of federal government spending goes to paying interest on the debt. Even though the debt has recently been increasing as a percent of GDP, interest rates were at historic lows in 2010–2011. Therefore interest payments as a percent of GDP have remained in line with those over the past 40 years. And recall that much of the interest payment comes in the form of transfer payments from U.S. taxpayers to U.S. bondholders. Nevertheless, the interest payments are large, and this mean that the government cannot spend the money on other programs. If the interest payments on the debt grow, paying the interest on the debt could involve higher taxes, which may decrease both aggregate demand and aggregate supply in the future.

Burden on Future Generation

An often-heard criticism of the national debt is that it imposes burdens on future generations. If at some point we decide to pay off the debt, future generations will have to decrease spending to pay off the bonds as they become due. This means, for example, that people 30 years from now will have to sacrifice consumption to pay back the bonds that were sold today. But in addition to inheriting the debt, future generations also inherit the bonds themselves, which are an asset.

How much of a burden today's debt places on future generations depends in part on what the bonds were used for when they were sold initially. For example, if money is borrowed today to improve roads or bridges or to defend the country against foreign enemies, it is likely that people living 30 years from today will benefit from this spending as do those people living today. Most people would agree that the deficit spending in WWII to defend the United States and its allies against foreign enemies was well spent. Thus the burden of the debt on future generations is decreased future consumption less the benefits derived from the spending when the debt was incurred. If spending today is on things that do not benefit people in the future, the repayment will be a greater burden overall.

Foreign-held Debt

When people, businesses, or governments from other countries buy U.S. bonds, they are lending money to the U.S. government to finance spending on goods and services. This is beneficial because it allows for increased spending in the United States when the bonds are initially purchased. However, the interest payments that are made on this foreign-held or external debt go to people abroad. The interest payments on the foreign-held debt generally do not benefit the U.S. economy directly. However, since the interest is paid in U.S. dollars, some of the dollars would likely be used to purchase U.S. exports and assets.

Moreover, there is the possibility that foreigners will not want to hold U.S. bonds indefinitely. This is especially a problem if they believe that the U.S. government will default on the interest that is due on the bonds or will fail to pay back the money that it borrowed. This possibility became a problem in the summer of 2011 when Congress stalled in reaching an agreement on raising the debt ceiling. If foreign bonds become due and new bonds are not sold to foreigners, this can impose a burden on future generations. The money that is repaid goes outside of the United States. On the other hand, like interest payments, because the money repaid when bonds mature is paid in U.S. dollars, some of the dollars would likely be used to purchase U.S. exports and assets.

Inflation

It is often stated that in the long run, the national debt is inflationary. An increase in government spending from borrowing increases aggregate demand and can put upward pressure on prices. In the long run, in order for inflation to be sustained, the money supply must grow faster than the rate of growth of output or GDP. If the government sells bonds to businesses, individuals, or the foreign sector, the money supply does not change. The government has money from selling the bonds, and the bond buyer has a bond and not the money. However, if the government sells bonds directly to the Federal Reserve, this does increase the money supply and could be inflationary if measures are not taken to offset the inflationary pressures. The role of the money supply and the Federal Reserve will be discussed in Chapter 8.

Crowding Out

Recall that crowding out occurs if government borrowing causes higher interest rates and the higher interest rates result in decreased private investment. This may offset the effects of an expansionary fiscal policy, but because it involves government borrowing, crowding out may also be viewed as a problem related to the national debt.

Higher interest rates from government borrowing are not desirable for either the government or the private sector because these higher rates mean that the government has to pay more interest on the debt. Increased interest rates mean that it is more expensive for private businesses and individuals to borrow. Moreover, crowding out means that the government sector of the economy is growing at the expense of the private sector. In a market-based economy, few would consider this to be a desirable outcome. Even if government investment is as large as the crowded-out private investment, so there is no overall decline in investment, many would argue that we do not want government investment to replace private investment.

There is a lack of consensus about the extent to which crowding out occurs. When interest rates are very low (as they were in 2010–2011), it may appear that crowding out is not occurring. But because the Federal Reserve was engaging in extraordinary measures to keep interest rates low during this time to deal with the financial crisis, the effects of the increased deficits on interest rates and private borrowing may surface later.

The Bottom Line

Today there is widespread concern about the growing deficits and growing national debt in the U.S. economy. Part of this concern centers around whether the debt can be sustained over the long run. This depends on the continued willingness of people to buy U.S. government bonds to finance the debt. Assessing the burden of the debt involves evaluating benefits from government borrowing against what might have happened had the borrowing not occurred.

Although some of the perceived burdens of the debt are probably not as great as is often believed, decreasing deficits and eventually decreasing the debt could certainly ease some of the burdens caused by the debt today and in the future. There are political differences about how and when this debt reduction should take place. Some believe higher taxes should be levied on the rich, whereas others believe deficit reduction should come entirely from spending cuts. Whether the deficit should be reduced while the country is still recovering from the financial crisis and the recession of December 2007–June 2009 is also a matter of controversy.

SUMMARY

When the economy is facing problems with inflation, unemployment, or sluggish growth, the government can engage in fiscal policy to address these problems. The tools of fiscal policy are changing taxes and government spending. Some fiscal policy is discretionary, whereas other fiscal policy takes place automatically because of existing laws. In theory, fiscal policy should result in multiplier effects on aggregate demand, however the actual impact of the multiplier is much smaller than expected. Supply-side fiscal policy emphasizes tax decreases intended to increase incentives to work and produce, which then increases aggregate supply. There are several problems associated with the way fiscal policy operates, including timing problems and crowding out.

The national debt is the sum of the annual budget deficits of the federal government over time, minus the surpluses. The government finances the debt by selling bonds to borrow money. Most of the debt is held by government agencies and U.S. businesses and individuals, but about one-third is held by foreigners. Although some of the perceived problems of the national debt are not as great as they might first appear to be, most people believe that annual deficits and the national debt should be reduced.

Further Reading

Barro, Robert J., and Charles J. Redlick. "Stimulus Spending Doesn't Work." *The Wall Street Journal*. 2009. Retrieved online September 2011 at http://online.wsj.com/article/SB1 0001424052748704447150457444072329878 6310.html.

Congressional Budget Office. http://www.cbo.gov/.

"The Debt to the Penny and Who Holds It." U.S. Treasury Department. Retrieved online September 2011 at http://www.treasurydirect.gov/NP/BPDLogin?application=np.

Office of Management and Budget. www.whitehouse.gov/OMB. Retrieved online February 2012

Ownership of Federal Debt. 9/21/2011. U.S. Government Accounting Office. Retrieved online September 2011 at http://www.gao.gov/special.pubs/longterm/debt/owner ship.html.

"Ownership of Federal Securities." *Treasury Bulletin*. September 2011. Retrieved online September 2011 at http://www.fms.treas.gov/bulletin/b2011_3ofs.doc.

"Senate Passes $787 Billion Stimulus Bill." February 15, 2009. CNNMoney.com. Retrieved online September 2011 at http://money.cnn.com/2009/02/13/news/economy/house_ final_stimulus/index.htm.

Shim, Jae K., and Joel G. Siegel. *Dictionary of Economics*. New York: John Wiley & Sons, 1995.

"Taking Apart the Federal Budget." *Washington Post*. Retrieved online February 2012 at http://www.washingtonpost.com/wp-srv/special/politics/budget-2010/.

CHAPTER 7

MONEY AND
THE U.S. BANKING SYSTEM

If asked what economics is all about, a lot of people would respond "money." Although economics is a broad subject covering a lot of topics, studying economics does indeed involve learning about money. In fact, money is the focus of this chapter and the following chapter of this book. So what exactly is money? In this chapter we will address what money is, what money does, why money is different from other things, what people did before money existed, and the connection between money and banks.

WHAT IS MONEY?

When people in the United States think about money, most probably picture dollar bills and coins printed and minted by the U.S. Treasury. But the distinguishing characteristic of money is not its appearance or the fact that the government prints it or mints it or declares that it is legal tender. In economics, **money** is anything that is generally accepted in payment for goods and services or in the repayment of debts. Think about it this way: Which piece of paper would you prefer to have: a dollar bill with a picture of George Washington on it or a picture of your favorite sports star from a magazine? Your answer is likely to be the dollar bill, because the dollar has more value. And why does it have value? Because you know that other people will accept that dollar in payment for something. It is the general acceptability of the dollar as a form of payment that makes the dollar function as money. And this acceptability for payment is what makes money unique.

Sometimes people use the word money to refer to things besides something that enables people to purchase something. You have no doubt heard people say things like "He makes a lot of money." In this case, money refers to income. Or perhaps you've heard someone say, "Her family has a lot of money." In this case, money refers to wealth. This discussion, however, will focus on money as something that is widely accepted in payment for goods and services. It is important to note that what may function as money in one place may not work somewhere else. For example, if you wanted to go out for lunch in Indonesia, you would have to pay in Indonesian rupiah instead of dollars. You would have to exchange dollars for rupiah to pay for your lunch.

The Problem with Barter

How would you get goods and services that you did not produce yourself if there were no money? The answer to this question is that you could trade directly for goods and services. **Barter** means trading goods and services without money. In a barter economy, goods and services are exchanged for each other. For example, if you lived in a barter economy and you wanted to buy food, you might offer to trade your watch for the food or perhaps offer to perform some service, such as washing dishes.

Bartering, however, can be inconvenient. For example, suppose I grow artichokes and you are a dentist. If I want dental services, I would need to trade artichokes to you. Now suppose you do not want artichokes, but you want someone to cut your grass. To get dental services from you I would either have to offer to cut the grass myself, something I may not be able to do very well, or I could find someone who cuts grass and is willing to accept artichokes in payment. Then I would try to set up a three-way exchange. But this option presents its own difficulties because it may not be easy to find a grass-cutter who wanted artichokes.

Another problem with barter is that it can be difficult to establish the value of the goods and services traded. How many artichokes are worth a trip to the dentist, or what is the lawn-cutting price of an artichoke? A barter economy requires establishing values of goods and services in terms of many other goods and services.

Compared to barter, money makes an economy more efficient because it makes an economy run more smoothly. Returning to the dental services-artichokes-lawn cutting scenario, what if instead of barter there were a form of compensation that everyone accepted—i.e., money? I could sell my artichokes for money and then use that money to pay you, the dentist, for the dental services I need. You could then use that money to pay someone to cut your grass. And the prices of all goods and services could be expressed in advance in terms of money—so many dollars per bushel of artichokes, so many dollars for a root canal, and so many dollars for mowing and trimming a lawn.

Another way that the existence of money makes the economy more efficient compared to barter is that it encourages specialization. **Specialization** means that people produce one or a few goods and services, rather than producing everything for themselves. When people specialize in producing things they are good at producing, more gets produced at lower costs. People are more likely to specialize in a money economy than in a barter economy. In a barter economy, everyone would be more likely to provide for their own food, shelter, and other necessities in case they could not find anyone willing to trade for the things they needed for survival.

The Functions of Money

When you think about how inconvenient a barter economy would be, you can begin to understand and appreciate the functions of money in an economy. The three main functions of money are listed in the sidebar and are discussed in greater detail below.

Medium of Exchange

When money functions as a **medium of exchange**, it makes trading easier. People are willing to sell goods and services in exchange for dollars. They know that they can use the dollars to buy other goods and services, because other people will accept dollars too. It is easier to trade in exchange for dollars than for artichokes, dental services, or lawn-cutting services.

Unit of Account

If someone asked you how much something was worth, you would probably reply in terms of a dollar amount. In this case money is serving as a **unit of account,** which means that you are using money to express the value of something. You might say that your car is worth $10,000, or that you paid $10 for a scarf and $1 per pound for tomatoes. Expressing the value of things in terms of money enables you to quickly understand and compare the value of different goods and services.

Store of Value

If you get paid in money today, you can usually save that money and spend it at a later date. When this occurs, money serves as a **store of value**. For example, think

The Functions of Money

- Medium of Exchange
- Unit of Account
- Store of Value

about the difference between being paid with money and being paid with a fish. If you collected your pay in fish, it would not serve as a good store of value. You would not be able to save the fish and use it to buy something later, because fish does not last very long and has to be consumed or discarded relatively quickly.

Money is not the only thing that serves as a store of value. Other assets such as stocks, bonds, gold, or real estate can serve as a store of value. You can purchase these assets and sell them later. But these other assets do not also serve as a medium of exchange or as a unit of account. On the other hand, money does not always serve as a good store of value, and this is one reason why people invest in other assets. In periods of inflation, money loses value. When inflation rates are high, people have incentives to hold assets other than money if they think the prices of those assets will keep up with inflation.

How Do We Measure Money?

The amount of money in the economy, or the money supply, is important for several reasons. It influences aggregate (total) demand in the economy. The money supply affects how much banks have to lend and affects consumption and investment. Too much money can cause inflation, and too little money can cause unemployment and a decline in GDP. Because the money supply is important, we need to know what is included in the money supply and how it is measured.

The money supply is measured by the Federal Reserve (the Fed), the U.S. central bank. There are two main measures of the money supply: M1 and M2. The sidebar shows what is included in M1 and M2. **M1** basically comprises currency in circulation and checking-type deposits. Travelers' checks are included too, but they represent a very small percentage of the total. **Currency** (cash) includes both paper money and coins. Currency in circulation refers to currency outside of banks. A **demand deposit** is a checking account that allows you to withdraw your money whenever you want to (on demand) without penalty. Other checkable deposits refers to accounts that allow you to withdraw your money by writing checks, but with some restrictions (e.g., how many checks you can write per month). M1 is the most narrow measure of the money supply because it includes the fewest things.

If asked how much money you have, you would probably include money in your savings account as well as cash you keep on hand and money in your checking account. **M2** is a broader measure of the money supply than M1 because it includes M1 and deposits in small savings-type accounts. In this case "small" means savings accounts with balances of under $100,000. A **time deposit** is a type of savings account that pays interest for a certain period of time, such as one year or three years. A **money market mutual fund** is a type of savings account that pools the savings of many people and invests in short-term debt securities such as Treasury bills and pays interest to savers.

What Is Included in M1 and M2?

(June 2011: Billions of dollars seasonally adjusted)

M1	$1,947.4
Currency in circulation	967.5
Demand deposits	574.6
Other checkable deposits	402.9
Travelers' checks	4.5

M2	$9,111.4
M1	1947.4
Savings deposits	5,628.5
Small-denomination time deposits	841.3
Money market mutual funds	701.7

(Note that individual components do not add to M1 and M2 totals due to rounding.)
Source: Federal Reserve H.6 Release

The savings account parts of M2 are not as liquid as the components of M1. **Liquidity** is the ability to convert something into cash. The more liquid something is, the easier it is to convert into cash. Cash is the most liquid asset. Checks are very liquid because they can be used like cash to pay for something. Money in savings accounts is not quite as liquid because you have to withdraw money from your savings account before you can use it to buy something. A credit card is not considered money, even though you can use it to purchase things. This is because you pay your credit card bill with currency or a check.

MONEY THROUGH HISTORY
Types of Money

Barter economies preceded economies with money. But as explained above, bartering can be difficult because you have to find someone willing to trade for what you have. No one knows precisely when money was first used, but we do know that it has been around for a long time. The concept and use of money no doubt evolved over time in different parts of the world to facilitate exchanges of goods and services. As shown in the sidebar, cattle and other forms of live-stock may have been the first form of money and were used as early as 9000 B.C. (www.pbs.org). As agriculture developed, grain and other plant products served as money. The Egyptians used metal rings as money in 2500 B.C. (www.min-neapolisfed.org). Cowrie shells, found in the Pacific and Indian Oceans, were used as money in China as early as 1200 B.C. Bronze and copper were made into early coins in China at the end of the Stone Age; these coins often had holes and could be hung on chains. Modern round metal coins made of precious metals appeared in Lydia (which is today part of Turkey) around 500 B.C. During the next few centuries, the use of metal coins spread to Greece, Rome, and other countries. Leather squares with decorated borders were used as money in China around 118 B.C. China was also the first country to use paper money, which was first introduced during the T'ang Dynasty, which ruled the country from 618 to 907 A.D. Other items that have served as money include beads, tobacco, tea, and furs. Prior to and following European settlement in North America, native Americans used money called wampum—strings of beads made from clam shells.

Money and Payments Systems

We can further investigate the history of money by looking at how methods of making payments have changed over time. Barter was the earliest form of pay-ment. The next widely used form of payment was **commodity money**, which is money that has intrinsic value. This means that the good that was being used as money had value in and of itself. Cattle is an example of commodity money, but the most commonly used commodity money was precious metals such as gold, silver, and copper. The metals had value themselves, and when they were made into coins, the value of the coin depended on the value of the metal it was made from.

Examples of Money in Early Times

Dates in parentheses indicate the approximate time when a particular form of money first came into general use.

- Cattle (9000 B.C.)
- Metal rings (2500 B.C.)
- Cowrie shells (1200 B.C.)
- Metal money and coins (1000 B.C.)
- Modern coins (500 B.C.)
- Leather money (118 B.C.)
- Paper currency (806 A.D.)

Source: www.pbs.org/ and www.minneapolisfed.org/

The Evolution of Payments Systems

- Barter
- Commodity Money
- Representative Money and Checks
- Fiat Money
- E-Money

Another payment system involves writing checks. The story of how checking accounts might have come to be involves a goldsmith in a time when precious metals such as gold were circulating as money. One problem with this was that people had to carry the gold around if they set out to buy things. Aside from the fact that gold is heavy, there was always the possibility of theft or loss. For all these reasons, some people decided to deposit their gold with the local goldsmith for safekeeping. The goldsmith would give them a receipt in exchange for the gold on deposit.

Eventually, people realized that they could use the goldsmith's receipts to buy things, and thus the deposit receipt became money. The receipts were a form of **representative money,** which means that they represented and could be exchanged for a certain amount of gold. The receipts operated much like checks do today. For example, if you write a check to buy a car, you are telling your bank to pay the car seller some of your money. In the era of the goldsmith's story, if someone paid for a horse with a gold receipt, this was telling the goldsmith that the horse seller now owned the gold.

Fiat money is money that the government declares is money. It is not convertible into a fixed amount of gold, silver, or other assets. The dollar bills (Federal Reserve Notes) that circulate as money in the United States today are examples of fiat money. These bills have value because of their official acceptability. You are willing to be paid in dollars because you know that you can use those dollars to buy things because other people are willing to accept them as payment.

Today, many payments are made electronically without any actual money changing hands. Electronic money, or **e-money**, can take the place of both checks and cash. A payment made with a debit card is an example of e-money. Money is transferred electronically from a buyer's account to a seller's account. Smart cards are another example of e-money. You load a certain amount of money from your bank account to a smart card and then use the card to purchase things.

Desirable Characteristics of Money

The discussion on types of money and types of payment systems has perhaps made you think about what makes some things function as money better than others. Historically, for example, why did gold and silver circulate as money rather than sand or ice? And if you were designing money for an economy today, what would that money be like? The sidebar lists some desireable characteristics for money.

One thing that comes to mind when we think about desirable characteristics of money is that we would like money to be durable or storable, so that it can help to serve the function of money as a store of value. If something does not last long, it is unlikely to be accepted in payment because it cannot be used to buy something else later on.

It is also helpful if money is portable or easy to carry. If money is too bulky or too heavy, it can make it difficult to use as a medium of exchange. One interesting exception to this concept of portability is the large stone disks that served as money on the Yap islands in the South Pacific. The largest of these were 12 feet in diameter and weighed thousands of pounds. These stones had holes in the middle and could technically be moved, but actual possession of the stones was often unnecessary because people knew who owned them. In addition to not being portable, these large and heavy disks also lack another desirable feature of money—divisibility. It is helpful to be able to divide money into parts so that it can purchase different quantities of things. For example, if your only currency were $100 bills, it would be difficult to buy a pack of gum.

It is also important that money be recognizable. For example, if every state in the US had its own currency, it could be difficult to recognize what was legitimate money and what was not. If someone offered to pay you with money from another state and you were not sure if it was really money, you will not accept it in payment. Money should also be scarce, and the supply should be controllable. If anyone could go to the beach and find clam shells that functioned as money, the money would not be scarce. Moreover, the supply of clam shell money and prices could rise and fall with the uncontrollable tides.

Another desirable feature of money is that it should be difficult to counterfeit. **Counterfeit money** is money that has been produced illegally. Unfortunately, counterfeiting is easier today than it was in the past due to the improved quality and availability of printers and scanners. The U.S. Treasury

Criteria for "Good" Money

- Durable
- Portable
- Divisible
- Recognizable
- Scarce
- Difficult to counterfeit

Department frequently redesigns currency to try to make it more secure against counterfeiting.

The Role of Gold

Historically, of all the precious metals, gold has had the most significant role. People have fought and died to maintain stores of gold. Gold was used to make decorative objects as early as 4000 B.C. and in 3000 B.C. was used to make jewelry in what today is southern Iraq (www.nma.org). Gold has been valued for ornamental purposes but also because it has been widely considered to be valuable by others.

In 1284 A.D. both Venice and Great Britain issued popular gold coins, and in 1377 Great Britain began basing its system of money on silver and gold. Early explorers, including Christopher Columbus, were searching for gold. Government-sponsored expeditions, especially by the Spanish in the 1500s, plundered native American civilizations of their gold. The Spanish believed that the country with the largest stockpile of gold would be the most powerful country.

The first U.S. gold coin was made in 1787, and in 1792 the United States set the value of the U.S. dollar in fixed amounts of gold and silver. The Gold Standard Act of 1900 put the United States on an official gold standard and this meant that paper money could be exchanged for a fixed amount of gold, but not silver. In 1913, the Federal Reserve Act required that the paper Federal Reserve Notes had to be backed by 40 percent of their value in gold. In 1934 President Roosevelt established the official value of gold at $35 per ounce. At this point U.S. citizens could no longer hold monetary gold, and no more gold coins were minted.

Following World War II, the Bretton Woods Agreement set up a system sometimes called the gold exchange standard. It also established the International Monetary Fund and the World Bank. The gold exchange standard meant that the value of the dollar and other currencies were defined in terms of gold internationally and that countries were obligated to exchange gold for their currencies held by other countries.

Between 1968 and 1971, the United States stopped backing Federal Reserve Notes with gold and also stopped exchanging foreign-held dollars for gold. Soon after, major world currencies began to "float," meaning that their values were now determined by supply and demand and not by the amount of gold held or the price of gold. As of 1974, Americans could purchase gold for investment purposes in forms other than jewelry. Today, some people choose to purchase gold as an investment and as a store of value, hoping that its value will increase. Although gold has played an important monetary role throughout history, it is important to recognize that the U.S. dollar is not tied to gold today. The dollar has value today, not because of any relationship with gold, but because it is widely accepted in payment.

THE U.S. BANKING SYSTEM

We now turn to a discussion of the U.S. banking system and the role of banks in the economy. The Federal Reserve System, the U.S. central bank, will be discussed in Chapter 8. Banks are important to the operation of an economy because they help to transfer funds from those who have money to save to those who want to borrow. In this sense, banks are financial intermediaries. A **financial intermediary** is an institution that receives deposits from savers and lends the funds to borrowers.

Think how different it would be if you wanted to save money and earn some interest on your savings if there were no banks. How could you locate a trustworthy person who wanted to borrow your money and who would pay you interest in exchange? Or what if you wanted to borrow money? How could you find someone willing to lend you money and charge you a reasonable amount of interest? Knowing that there are banks that you can trust makes the saving and borrowing process work more smoothly, and makes the economy run more smoothly in general.

People's faith in the banking system is important for a well-functioning economy. If you worry that a bank is going to fail, you will not deposit money there. Most deposit accounts today are insured so that depositors can trust their banks and know that their deposits are safe. For example, deposits in banks and many thrift institutions are insured up to $250,000 by the Federal Deposit Insurance Corporation, the FDIC (www.fdic.gov). Deposits in federal credit unions and most state credit unions are insured up to $250,000 by the National Credit Union Administration (www.ncua.gov).

Types of Banks

There are different types of banks that perform many of the same functions. **Commercial banks** are the all-purpose banks that you probably think of when you hear the word "bank." Commercial banks offer a variety of services such as checking accounts, time and savings accounts, business loans, and mortgage loans. Some offer student loans and also sell insurance, stocks, and bonds. **Thrifts** and thrift institutions are terms used for credit unions, savings banks, and savings and loan banks. Today these institutions perform many of the same functions as commercial banks, but they are more likely to specialize in time deposits and mortgages. **Credit unions** are a type of thrift institution that requires membership. Credit unions often charge members lower interest on loans and pay higher interest on savings than other types of banks.

How Banks Create Money

It may sound strange to say that banks can create money. After all, it is the U.S. Treasury that prints money—not banks. So what do we mean when we say that banks create money? To answer this question we have to recall that the M1 money supply consists of checking account balances as well as currency in circulation. Banks create money because they are able to make loans in the form of checking accounts. Understanding this process will help you understand the role of the Federal Reserve in the economy, the topic of the next chapter. But an understanding of how banks create money requires some information about the operation of the Federal Reserve.

Say that you found $100 in your great-grandmother's old cookbook, and she tells you that you may keep it. You take this $100 to your bank and deposit it in your checking account. Does your bank keep this $100 in a little box with your name on it, so that it will be there if you want to withdraw it? The answer is "No." Your bank keeps a fraction of this $100 in reserves to back up your deposit, and then it can lend out the rest. This is called a **fractional reserve system of banking**. Banks do not have to keep the whole amount, or 100 percent, of deposits in reserve. The amount that banks have to keep in reserve to back up your deposit is set by the Federal Reserve. This is called the **reserve requirement**. Banks have to keep their reserves either in vault cash or on deposit with the Federal Reserve. **Excess reserves** are the amount of reserves that a bank has over and above the required reserves. Any bank can lend out the amount of its excess reserves.

Currently the reserve requirement is 10 percent against most checking account deposits. So your bank would hold $10 in reserves against your deposit of $100, and it could lend out the remaining $90. If the loan is in the form of currency or a deposit in a checking account, the bank has "created" $90 in new money. You still have your deposit of $100, and someone else has the $90 that was borrowed. But the process does not stop here. If the person who borrowed the $90 deposits the money into a checking account at a bank, that bank can now lend out its new excess reserves as well. This process is called multiple deposit creation or expansion.

The Money Multiplier Process

New money is generally injected into the system when the Federal Reserve buys bonds (instead of finding money in an old book). This increases the amount of reserves that banks have. For example, assume that the Fed has purchased a $10,000 bond from Bank A. The Fed pays the bank $10,000, which the bank deposits. Bank A now has $10,000 in excess reserves. We trace the money creation process from this initial injection of reserves into the banking system in Table 7.1. The table is designed with the underlying assumption that banks wish to lend out all of their excess reserves and that bank customers wish to keep all of their money in the form of demand deposits rather than in currency.

Because of the Fed's actions, Bank A has $10,000 in excess reserves in round 1. Assume that the bank makes a loan to you for $10,000 by depositing the money into your checking account. Because checking deposits are part of the money supply, the money supply has increased by $10,000. The bank must keep $1,000 (10 percent) in required reserves to back up your checking account and now has $9,000 in excess reserves (round 2 in Table 7.1). The bank can therefore lend out the $9,000 in excess reserves. This loan could remain in Bank A or it could be deposited into another bank. Regardless, in round 3 the banking system must keep $900 in required reserves to back up the $9,000 deposit and can loan out the $8,100 in excess reserves. When the $8,100 in excess reserves is deposited into a checking account (round 4), the money supply increases by this amount. The bank with the deposit must hold $810 in required reserves and can loan out the excess reserves of $7,290 (round 5).

TABLE 7.1

How Banks Create Money: Deposit Expansion Process

(Assume: reserve requirement is 10 percent, that banks lend out all of their excess reserves, and that the public holds demand deposits rather than currency.)

Round:	Increase in Money Supply (demand deposits)	Required Reserves	Excess Reserves
1			$10,000
2	$10,000	$1,000	$9,000
3	$9,000	$900	$8,100
4	$8,100	$810	$7,290
5	$7,290	$729	$6,561
Continue this process	(continue)	(continue)	(continue)
Total of all rounds:	$100,000	$10,000	$90,000

Fig 7.1 M1 Money Multiplier

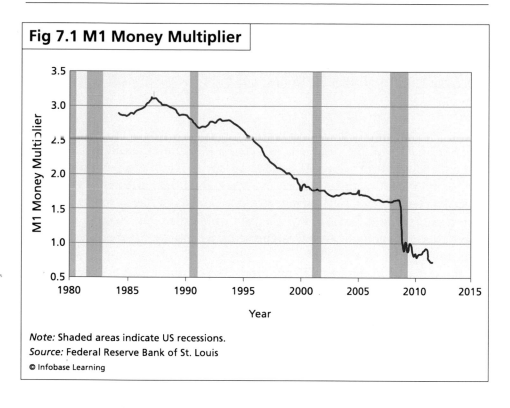

Note: Shaded areas indicate US recessions.
Source: Federal Reserve Bank of St. Louis
© Infobase Learning

Although all the subsequent rounds are not shown in Table 7.1, this process would continue. In the end, based on a reserve requirement of 10 percent and an initial injection of new money of $10,000, the money supply could increase by as much as $100,000. This process is called the money multiplier process or the deposit expansion process. The **money multiplier** tells us how much money will be created from excess reserves. In this case the money multiplier is 10, because an increase in excess reserves of $10,000 has generated an increase in the money supply of $100,000. Ten is the maximum possible money multiplier with a reserve requirement of 10 percent. The money multiplier is also called the deposit expansion multiplier. A simple formula shows how the money multiplier works:

Change in money supply = money multiplier x change in excess reserves

In reality, banks do not loan out all of their excess reserves and people choose to hold some of M1 in the form of currency, so the actual money multiplier is far lower than 10. As shown in Figure 7.1, the money multiplier from 1955 through 2011 ranged from a little over three to less than one. It fell following the financial crisis that began in 2007 and the recession that lasted from

December 2007 through June 2009. During this period, banks were holding many excess reserves rather than risking making loans that could not be repaid, and this decreased the money multiplier. The figure shows that the money multiplier also fell during other recessions.

SUMMARY

Money plays an important role in any economy. Money avoids the inconvenience of barter and serves the functions of being a medium of exchange, a unit of account, and a store of value. M1 and M2 are the Federal Reserve's official measures of money. Throughout history, many commodities have served as money, especially precious metals. However, gold does not play a role as money, or back money, in the United States today. The payments system has evolved over time from barter to commodity money, representative money, fiat money, and electronic money.

The U.S. banking system is an important part of the U.S. economy. There are different types of banks, including commercial banks and thrift institutions. Banks are able to create money in the economy when they make loans in the form of checking-type deposits. A single bank can loan out the amount of its excess reserves. For the banking system as a whole, the ability to create money can expand beyond the value of an initial loan through the money multiplier process.

Further Reading

Federal Reserve Statistical Release H.6. Money Stock Measures. Retrieved online August 2011 at http://www.federalreserve.gov/releases/h6/current/.

The History of Gold. The National Mining Association. Retrieved online August 2011 at http://www.nma.org/pdf/gold/gold_history.pdf.

The History of Money. The Federal Reserve Bank of Minneapolis. Retrieved online August 2011 at www.minneapolisfed.org/community_education/teacher/history.cfm.

The History of Money. Nova. Retrieved online August 2011 at www.pbs.org/wgbh/nova/ancient/history-money.html.

M1 Money Multiplier. Economics Research: Federal Reserve Bank of St. Louis. Retrieved online August 2011 at http://research.stlouisfed.org/fred2/series/MULT.

CHAPTER 8

THE FEDERAL RESERVE, MONETARY POLICY, AND FINANCIAL CRISES

When you think of a bank, you probably think of the place where you have your checking account or savings account. It is probably located close to where you live or work. But there is another type of bank that is very important for the economy: the central bank. The Federal Reserve System is the name of the central bank of the United States. The Federal Reserve System is also called the Federal Reserve or simply the Fed. (But note that it is not the same as "the feds," which refers to people who are agents of a federal government agency or bureau.) Why do we need a central bank? How is the Federal Reserve System organized, and what functions does it perform? What is monetary policy, and how does the Federal Reserve implement it to try to stabilize the economy? What does the Fed do if there is a financial crisis? These are some of the questions addressed in this chapter.

EARLY CENTRAL BANKING IN THE UNITED STATES

Throughout its history, the United States has been skeptical of central power. Despite this wariness, Alexander Hamilton, the first Secretary of the Treasury, recognized the need for a central bank. A central bank could stimulate the economy, improve the credit of the government, make loans to the government, serve as the bank of the government, provide a uniform currency, and regulate state banks. Following Hamilton's advice, the First Bank of the United States was created and received a 20-year charter in 1791. Although the First Bank of the United States is viewed as a successful institution that made a positive impact on the economy, its charter was not renewed in 1811. Opponents, who favored fewer centralized institutions, believed that the bank was representative of strong central government (http://eh.net).

Because there was no central bank after 1811, the U.S. government had trouble financing the costs of the War of 1812. Partly for this reason, a second central bank was established, and in 1816, this Second Bank of the United States received a 20-year charter from Congress. With Nicholas Biddle as its director and later as its president, the bank sold government bonds and served as a repository for the government to deposit funds. It provided credit for businesses and also provided a reliable paper currency. By requiring state banks to hold reserves, the Second Bank of the United States helped to inspire confidence in the nation's banking system. Andrew Jackson, who served as President of the United States from 1829 to 1837, strongly opposed the Second Bank of the United States. Among other things, he objected to its centralized power and control. Jackson withdrew government funds from the bank in 1833, and the bank's charter was not renewed in 1836 (sss.cr.nps.gov/history/).

Subsequent administrations did not reverse this policy and as a result, the United States did not have a central bank from 1836 to 1913. This meant that the country had no institution that could serve in the role of lender of last resort to commercial banks. When the central bank serves in the role of **lender of last resort**, it lends money to banks when no one else is willing or able to do so. This function is important if a bank is having temporary problems but is otherwise sound. With no lender of last resort, commercial banks were subject to failure due to bank panics. A **bank panic** occurs when depositors are worried that the bank holding their deposits will fail, so they withdraw their deposits in the form of cash. Because banks do not hold enough cash to back up 100 percent of deposits, they do not have enough cash to pay everyone if all depositors decide to withdraw at the same time. With no lender of last resort to provide cash loans to the banks, many banks will fail if there is a panic. And without deposit insurance, depositors will lose their money.

The United States suffered a series of financial panics in the late 19th and early 20th centuries, specifically in 1873, 1884, 1893, and 1907. The Panic of 1907 was especially severe and led to the failure of many banks and other businesses throughout the country. The bank panics underscored the instability of the U.S. financial system and led to renewed discussions of the need for a central bank. The Federal Reserve Act was passed and became law in December 1913. This act created the Federal Reserve System, the name of the current central bank of the United States.

The Federal Reserve Act set up a system of 12 banks located throughout the country, rather than just one bank in one location. Establishing a system of 12 banks was a response to objections by some members of Congress that one central bank would represent the interests of people and businesses in the area in which that one bank was located and not the rest of the country. The original functions of the Federal Reserve were to serve as a lender of last resort to the commercial banking system and to control the amount of currency available to the economy.

FUNCTIONS OF THE FEDERAL RESERVE SYSTEM TODAY

The sidebar lists the major functions of the Fed today. One thing that the Fed does is issue currency to banks. The Fed does not print the money; this is done by the Bureau of Printing and Engraving in the U.S. Treasury Department. Once printed, the money is distributed to the 12 Federal Reserve banks, which then distribute it to commercial banks and thrifts. The Federal Reserve also clears checks written from one bank to another and from different Federal Reserve districts. For example, say that your uncle, who lives across the country, writes you a check for your birthday, and you deposit the check in your bank. The money gets transferred from his bank to yours through an electronic check-clearing process. The Fed subtracts the money from your uncle's bank and credits it to your bank.

You, as an individual or business, cannot have an account with the Fed. However, your bank can. Banks can make deposits with the Fed and keep reserves there, and they can also take out loans from the Fed. The Fed also serves as the bank of the federal government. The Fed regulates banks with the goal of making sure that they are financially sound and to ensure the stability of the banking system. As a regulatory agency, the Fed works to ensure competition in the banking industry and to protect consumers in banking matters. Other federal and state agencies also regulate banks.

Because the stability of the banking system is important, the Fed serves as a lender of last resort to banks that need to borrow. For banks to serve as

Functions of the Federal Reserve

- Issues currency
- Clears checks
- Serves as bank for commercial banks and thrift institutions
- Serves as bank for the federal government
- Supervises and regulates banks and thrift institutions
- Serves as lender of last resort
- Conducts monetary policy to stabilize the economy
- Conducts economic research

Fig 8.1 The Structure of the Federal Reserve System

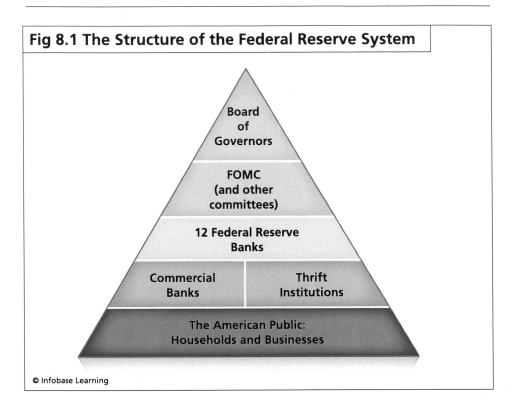

Board
of
Governors

FOMC
(and other
committees)

12 Federal Reserve
Banks

Commercial
Banks

Thrift
Institutions

The American Public:
Households and Businesses

© Infobase Learning

efficient financial intermediaries, it is important that people trust banks and know that their deposits are safe. The Fed, by serving as a lender of last resort, helps to accomplish this, as does deposit insurance provided by the FDIC. Although banks still fail today, depositors do not need to worry about losing their money if this happens. As noted in Chapter 7, the Federal Deposit Insurance Corporation (FDIC) insures deposits in banks and thrift institutions for at least $250,000. The FDIC was founded in 1933 after thousands of banks failed in the 1920s and 1930s, and many depositors lost their money. Since the FDIC began operations on January 1, 1934, no one has lost any money in an insured deposit (www.fdic.gov).

The most important function of the Federal Reserve is to conduct monetary policy to try to stabilize the economy. To help achieve this goal, each Federal Reserve bank employs economists who conduct research on monetary policy and other subjects. The website of the Board of Governors of the Federal Reserve (www.federalreserve.gov) and those of the twelve individual Reserve Banks are good sources of information for research and data about the economy.

ORGANIZATION AND STRUCTURE OF THE FEDERAL RESERVE

Figure 8.1 shows the organization of the Federal Reserve System. The main components of this organizational structure are the Board of Governors, the

Federal Open Market Committee, the 12 Federal Reserve banks, commercial banks and thrift institutions, and the households and businesses that make up the public. The members of the Board of Governors are the leaders of the Federal Reserve System. The board consists of seven people, who are appointed by the President and approved by the Senate. They serve 14-year terms and cannot be reappointed to another full term. The terms are staggered so that one term expires every other year. The chairman of the Board of Governors is appointed for a four-year term and can be reappointed within the 14-year term. The chairman (Ben Bernanke in 2011) serves as the country's spokesperson on monetary policy. Conducting monetary policy is the major function of the Board of Governors.

The Federal Open Market Committee, the FOMC, was established in 1935 and is the most important committee in the Federal Reserve System. There are 12 voting members: the seven members of the Board of Governors and five of the 12 Federal Reserve Bank presidents. The president of the Federal Reserve Bank of New York is always on the FOMC. The other four positions rotate among the remaining 11 Reserve Bank presidents. The FOMC meets eight times per year to make decisions about the future course of monetary policy in the

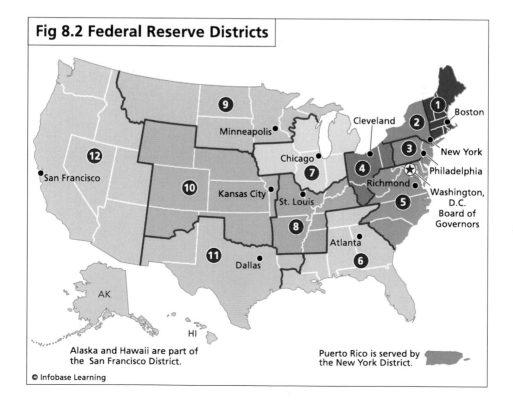

Fig 8.2 Federal Reserve Districts

Minneapolis
Cleveland
Boston
New York
Chicago
San Francisco
Philadelphia
Richmond
Kansas City
St. Louis
Washington, D.C.
Board of Governors
Atlanta
Dallas
AK
HI

Alaska and Hawaii are part of the San Francisco District.

Puerto Rico is served by the New York District.

© Infobase Learning

United States. If you hear on the news that the Fed is meeting, it means that the FOMC is meeting.

The United States is divided into 12 Federal Reserve districts, and each district has a Reserve Bank. (See Figure 8.2 for locations.) Banks and thrifts keep deposits with their local Reserve Bank and may be able to take out loans from their Reserve Bank. Reserve Banks are also involved in supervising banks in their district. Most of the banks are in the eastern half of the United States because when the Fed was formed in 1913, most of the population of the country was in the East.

The Reserve Banks also put currency in circulation. Have you ever noticed that the front of a dollar bill contains a letter within a circle? The letters range from A to L. There is also a number that appears four times on the front of the dollar bill (look for these near each number 1 in the four corners). These numbers range from 1 to 12. The letters and numbers tell you which Reserve Bank distributed the currency. For example, if you have a dollar bill with the letter B and number 2, it is from District 2, New York.

Commercial banks may become members of the Federal Reserve System. Today there are about 8,039 commercial banks in the United States, and about 38 percent of these are members of the Federal Reserve System (www.federal-reserveeducation.org). National banks, those that received their charters from the federal government, must be members. State-chartered banks may become members if they meet specified requirements. Member banks have stock in Reserve Banks and receive dividends.

In addition to commercial banks, there are about 12,000 thrift institutions that keep deposits in Reserve Banks. These thrift institutions include savings and loan associations, mutual savings banks, and credit unions. Commercial

Dollar bill embossed with the letter "B" and the number "2," on this bill tell us that the Federal Reserve Bank of New York put it into circulation.

banks and thrifts are both subject to Federal Reserve regulations and reserve requirements; in exchange, they receive services such as loans and check clearing. The households and businesses that comprise the non-bank public in the United States can take part in the banking system through accounts, loans, and other services available from commercial banks and thrifts.

INDEPENDENCE OF THE FEDERAL RESERVE SYSTEM

Although the Federal Reserve was created by an act of Congress and could therefore be eliminated by an act of Congress, it is quite independent from federal government control. In fact, the Federal Reserve System is one of the most independent central banks in the world. Unlike other federal agencies, it does not receive funding from the government. The Fed is funded through revenues earned on government bond holdings and from interest charged on loans to banks. Instead of receiving funding from the government, the Fed returns money to the U.S. Treasury every year. Because the Fed does not depend on government funding, it does not have to be concerned about Congressional decisions regarding appropriations. Another indicator of Fed independence is that when the Fed makes decisions about what to do for the economy, the decisions do not need to be approved by Congress or the President.

The 14-year rotating terms of the Board of Governors also make the Fed independent from the government. The 14-year terms span multiple presidential and congressional terms of office. The 14-year term is longer than any U.S. President can serve, and longer than the elected terms for both the Senate and the House of Representatives. Senators must stand for reelection every six years, and members of the House of Representatives stand for reelection every two years. Because of the 14-year rotating terms, the ability of any one President to appoint the majority of the Board of Governors is limited. As well, Reserve Bank Presidents are chosen by the Directors of each bank and not by politicians, another indicator of independence of the political process.

There are strong arguments in favor of having an independent central bank. Those supporting this independence argue that managing the money supply requires skilled experts who should be appointed for their financial expertise and not for political reasons. If a central bank is not independent from the government, then the jobs of the leaders of the bank could depend on having support from the politicians who are in office. This could mean that bank leaders might have incentives to conduct policies to help supportive politicians get reelected rather than to do what is best for the country. And this, in turn, would give monetary policy a more short-term focus.

There is strong international evidence that independent central banks lead to better outcomes for the economy. Several research studies have found that countries with central banks that are more independent have lower inflation, while countries with less independent central banks have relatively higher inflation.

Some people are against central bank independence, arguing that the leaders of the central bank should be responsible to the electorate, like the President and members of Congress. They point out that although monetary policy is highly technical and requires knowledgeable people to conduct it, other polices (such as foreign policy) are also highly technical but are nonetheless conducted by elected officials to some degree. Citing the Great Depression, critics of central bank independence also point out that the Fed has not always used its independence well, and that it has not been able to prevent other economic crises from occurring.

MONETARY POLICY

The most important function of the Federal Reserve System is conducting monetary policy. **Monetary policy** is defined as a central bank's changing the money supply to affect interest rates to achieve national goals. The goals of monetary policy are price stability, full employment, and having GDP reach its full-employment potential. Monetary policy tries to reduce the inflation and unemployment associated with the extremes of the business cycle and to achieve steady, sustainable economic growth.

The Tools of Monetary Policy: Traditional Tools

The Fed has several tools at its disposal to manage the nation's money supply. Three of these tools have been in place for a long time, and others have been developed to address the financial crisis that began in 2007. The Fed's traditional monetary policy tools are reserve requirements, the discount rate, and open market operations.

Reserve Requirements

Chapter 7 explained that banks and thrifts have to keep a certain amount of reserves to back up checking-type deposits. The reserve requirement, the amount banks must keep in reserves, is set by the Fed. Today reserves may be held as vault cash or as deposits with the Fed. Reserve requirements on most deposits (those above $58.8 million) are 10 percent. The reserve requirement is also called the reserve ratio because it is expressed as a percentage of checkable deposits. Banks have to meet reserve requirements every other Thursday.

If the Fed were to increase reserve requirements, banks would have to keep more in reserves and could make fewer loans. Recall that loans made to checking accounts increase the money supply. Increasing the reserve requirement would therefore be likely to decrease the money supply. If the Fed were to lower the reserve requirement, banks would have to keep less money in reserves and could make more loans. Because this would result in more deposits in checking

Reserve Requirements

Liability Type	Requirement	
	% of checking-type deposits	Effective date
Deposit Amount:		
$0 to $10.7 million	0 %	12-30-10
More than $10.7 million to $58.8 million	3 %	12-30-10
More than $58.8 million	10 %	12-30-10
Time deposits	0 %	12-27-90

Source: www.federalreserve.gov

accounts, this would likely increase the money supply. However, the Fed seldom changes the reserve requirement because it is considered to be a "harsh" policy tool. For example, if banks were not holding excess reserves and the reserve requirement were raised, it could be difficult for banks to comply.

The Discount Rate

The **discount rate** is the interest rate that the Fed charges to banks and thrift institutions when they borrow from the Fed. The discount rate is the only interest rate that the Fed sets directly. Since 2003, the Fed has had three discount rates: for primary credit, for secondary credit, and for seasonal credit. The primary credit rate is for banks that are in good financial condition but need temporary (overnight) loans. The secondary credit rate is higher and charged to banks that have financial problems and are not eligible for the primary credit rate. The seasonal rate is charged for loans to relatively small banks that have fluctuations in deposits and withdrawals of a seasonal nature, such as in agricultural areas. When people talk about "the" discount rate, they are generally referring to the primary credit rate.

If the Fed raises the discount rate, it becomes more expensive for banks to borrow from the Fed. This discourages banks from making loans to others, leading to a decline in the money supply. If the Fed lowers the discount rate, it becomes cheaper for banks to borrow from the Fed. Because money is more readily available to banks, this encourages banks to lend to others, and thus increases the money supply.

Discount Rates (October 2011)

Primary Credit	0.75%
Secondary Credit	1.25%
Seasonal Credit	0.20%

Source: http://www.frbdiscountwindow.org

Open Market Operations

Open market operations are the purchase and sale of U.S. government securities by the Federal Reserve System. The securities are government bonds, bills, and notes. Open market operations are the Fed's main tradtional monetary policy tool today. The Federal Open Market Committee decides how many government securities to buy or sell, and the directives are carried out by the Federal Reserve Bank of New York. This tool is called "open market" operations because the Fed buys and sells the securities on the open bond market, where other (i.e., non-Fed) bond buyers and sellers trade.

When the Fed buys bonds, it injects new money into the economy and increases the money supply. If, for example, the Fed bought a $10,000 bond from you, you would have a check for $10,000 and the Fed would have the bond. You would likely deposit this in your bank, which would increase bank reserves. Via the money multiplier process described in Chapter 7, the money supply could increase by more than $10,000. Note that if you sold your bond to someone other than the Fed—to your brother for example—this would not change the money supply. You would have $10,000 but your brother would not.

If the Fed sells bonds, it takes money out of the economy and decreases the money supply. For example, if you bought a $10,000 bond that the Fed was selling, you would write a check for $10,000 to pay for it. When the check cleared, this would decrease the amount of money in your bank account and the reserves in your bank. The Fed would have the $10,000, but this amount would be out of the banking system so the money supply would fall. Note again that if you bought a bond from someone other than the Fed—like your brother—the money supply would not change. Your bank would have $10,000 less but your brother's bank would have $10,000 more. The money supply changes only when the Fed buys or sells government securities.

The Fed uses open market operations to target an interest rate called the federal funds rate. The **federal funds rate** is the interest rate that banks charge each other for overnight loans. When the Fed buys bonds, it increases bank reserves, so there is less need for banks to borrow from one another. This causes the federal funds rate to fall. When the Fed sells bonds, it decreases bank reserves and causes the federal funds rate to rise. Other short-term interest rates often move in the same direction as the federal funds rate. Even though the Fed does not directly set interest rates other than the discount rate, it influences other interest rates through open market operations and the federal funds rate. In August 2011, the Fed's target for the federal funds rate was from 0 percent to .25 percent, and the federal funds rate was .25 percent.

Because the Fed keeps the federal funds rate below the discount rate today, banks have incentives to borrow from each other rather than from the Fed. However discount policy is still important because it ensures that the Fed can serve in the role of lender of last resort. But because the Fed cannot force banks to borrow, the Fed has more control over open market operations as a policy tool to influence the money supply than over discount loans. This is why open market operations are the principal traditional monetary policy tool used today.

The Tools of Monetary Policy: New Tools
Interest on Reserves

The Fed began to pay interest to banks on required and excess reserves in October 2008. This change is good for banks because they now earn interest on their reserves. The change is also good for the Fed because it serves as another tool of monetary policy that potentially gives them more control over the money supply. Specifically, paying interest on reserves (IOR) gives the Fed more control over the federal funds rate, which is necessary for the way open market operations are conducted today. The IOR in the fourth quarter of 2011 was .25 percent.

Before October 2008, banks held few excess reserves because excess reserves did not earn interest, and banks could earn interest by lending out the excess reserves. In 2008, however, the federal funds rate fell close to zero percent. Therefore there was no reason for banks to want to lend to other banks, and this resulted in their holding large amounts of excess reserves. Because this was occurring during a financial crisis, banks also held excess reserves as a precautionary measure. This unpredictable demand for excess reserves made it more difficult for the Fed to hit its target federal funds rate.

However, with IOR, the federal funds rate will logically not fall below the IOR rate. This is because banks would rather hold excess reserves and earn the IOR rate than lend to other banks at a lower rate. This gives the Fed control over the lower level of the federal funds rate, which it would not have without IOR. As the economy recovers from the financial crisis and the recession of 2008–2009, the Fed's increased control over the federal funds rate will also be helpful in preventing inflation. When the Fed increases the IOR rate, this will put upward pressure on other interest rates also, which will help to fight inflation.

Other New Tools of Monetary Policy

The Federal Reserve instituted other new monetary policy tools to address the financial crisis that began in 2007. The purpose of these tools was to provide liquidity to institutions so that the cost of borrowing would decrease for consumers and businesses. In other words, if banks and other financial institutions had more liquid assets, they could provide loans and credit to individuals and businesses at lower interest rates. This would increase aggregate demand, increase production and employment, and help the economy recover. Some of these programs have expired and have been replaced with others. To see current and expired tools of monetary policy, go to the homepage of the Board of Governors of the Federal Reserve System and click on Monetary Policy, and then on Policy Tools (http://www.federalreserve.gov/monetarypolicy/default.htm).

Expansionary and Contractionary Monetary Policy

Expansionary Monetary Policy

Expansionary monetary policy is intended to increase aggregate demand to address the problems of unemployment and declining or sluggish output that are associated with recessions. When the Fed wants to expand the economy, it takes steps to encourage banks to make more loans. Since checking-type deposits are a form of money, the increased loans increase the money supply. As the money supply rises, interest rates in the economy fall. Because investment spending is especially sensitive to interest rates, the fall in interest rates leads to increases in investment spending, which is part of aggregate demand. As aggregate demand increases, more goods and services are produced and purchased, jobs are created, and unemployment falls. Expansionary monetary policies also increase consumption by encouraging banks to lend to households.

Expansionary and Contractionary Monetary Policy: Traditional Tools

Expansionary (Increase money supply, decrease interest rates, increase aggregate demand)	Contractionary (Decrease money supply, increase interest rates, decrease aggregate demand)
Decrease reserve requirement	Increase reserve requirement
Decrease discount rate	Increase discount rate
Buy bonds to increase bank reserves and decrease the federal funds rate	Sell bonds to decrease bank reserves and increase the federal funds rate

The traditional tools of monetary policy that encourage bank lending and lead to increases in the money supply are reducing the reserve requirement, reducing the discount rate, and open market purchases of government securities. If the Fed reduced the reserve requirement, banks would have more money to lend. If the Fed reduced the discount rate, banks could borrow more cheaply from the Fed and so could lend more cheaply to others. If the Fed bought government bonds, the most common expansionary tool, this would result in increased reserves in banks, which banks could then lend out.

Contractionary Monetary Policy

Contractionary monetary policy is intended to decrease or slow the rate of growth of aggregate demand to address inflation. If the money supply grows faster than output, there is upward pressure on prices. When the Fed is concerned about inflation, it wants to reduce the money supply or reduce the rate of growth of the money supply. It does this by discouraging banks from making loans. Decreases in the money supply raise interest rates and decrease borrowing by investors and consumers, leading to lower aggregate demand. Reductions in aggregate demand take pressure off rising prices and lead to less inflation.

The traditional monetary policy tools that discourage bank lending and lead to decreases in the money supply are increases in the reserve requirement, increases in the discount rate, and open market sales of bonds. If the Fed were to raise reserve requirements, banks would have to hold more reserves and so would not be able to make as many loans. If the Fed were to raise the discount rate, it would be more expensive for banks to borrow from the Fed and would discourage banks from lending to others. When the Fed sells bonds through open market operations, the most common contractionary tool, this reduces bank reserves so banks do not have as much to lend out.

Problems with Conducting Monetary Policy

Listing and discussing the monetary policy tools that the Fed can use to try to stabilize the economy may make it seem as if conducting monetary policy is straightforward. However, there are several problems that can prevent monetary policy from working as expected, and a few of these problems will be discussed here. Because monetary policy does not always work as expected, some people advocate that it be conducted by rules rather than at the discretion of the Fed. This position is discussed in more detail in Chapter 9.

Timing Problems

One problem with monetary policy is that it is subject to timing problems. Monetary policy, like fiscal policy, has a recognition lag. It can take time for researchers and policy makers at the Fed to figure out what is going on in the economy and additional time to decide how to best address any problems. The decision lag, the time it takes for policy makers to decide what to do about a problem in the economy, is relatively short with monetary policy because the FOMC can meet and issue directives to buy and sell bonds whenever it wants. However, the effect lag, the time it takes for monetary policy to affect prices, output, and employment, can be long. Monetary policy that takes effect by first lowering short-term interest rates, then increasing investment, then leading to more production and less unemployment, takes time.

Lack of Symmetry
Another problem with monetary policy is that some research indicates that it works better when fighting inflation than when fighting recessions and unemployment. To fight inflation, the Fed can sell bonds, withdraw reserves from banks, and decrease the ability of banks to make loans. But fighting unemployment is trickier, because the Fed cannot force banks to lend out excess reserves. The Fed can buy bonds and increase reserves in banks, but if banks choose to hold onto excess reserves rather than lending them out (as they did in 2011), this reduces the effectiveness of expansionary monetary policy.

Goals and Targets
The Fed officially has a dual mandate to try to achieve maximum sustainable economic growth and price stability. This means that the overall goals of monetary policy are to decrease the problems of inflation and unemployment and to promote steady economic growth. But the Fed does not have direct control over inflation, unemployment, GDP, or growth. It does, however, have good control over the federal funds rate through IOR and because it can affect bank reserves. Prior to the financial crisis, the Fed conducted monetary policy largely by changing the federal funds rate, which affects the money supply and other short-term interest rates and ultimately inflation, unemployment, and GDP.

Historically economists have debated what the Fed should do to best reach its overall goals. Should it set targets for the money supply, or interest rates, or the rate of inflation? For years, the Fed had money supply targets rather than interest rate targets. It abandoned this strategy in 2000 because it appeared that the relationship between the money supply and the goals of monetary policy had broken down. Today, many developed countries, including New Zealand, Canada, and Sweden, have adopted specific inflation targets. Advocates of inflation targeting point out that this makes monetary policy goals more transparent and that policy makers can then be held responsible for meeting the goals.

FINANCIAL CRISES AND FED RESPONSE
There is no precise definition for the term **financial crisis**, although there is agreement about common characteristics of financial crises. Financial crises are also called economic crises. They often involve disturbances in financial markets, such as the stock market. Credit available to businesses and households is limited. Some financial crises result in a loss of confidence in a country's

currency, leading to a withdrawal of funds from that country. Financial crises are sometimes associated with panics, during which depositors withdraw money from banks or other institutions such as the stock market. In such cases, the value of the affected financial institutions or assets falls rapidly. Financial crises often lead to recessions and often spread to other countries.

Although the Fed was founded in 1913 in response to a series of financial crises, it has not been entirely successful in preventing economic or financial crises from occurring since that time. Nonetheless, its response to financial crises and its knowledge about how to prevent them from worsening has improved over time. The remainder of this chapter examines three financial crises that have occurred since the founding of the Fed and the way that the Fed responded to them.

The Great Depression

The Great Depression is the worst financial crisis to occur in the 20th century, both in the United States and throughout the industrialized world. It is often said to have lasted from the stock market crash of October 1929 to 1942, when GNP recovered to its pre-depression level. The NBER dates a recession as having occurred from August 1929 to March 1933, followed by an expansion, and then another contraction from May 1937 to June 1938. Because the contraction of 1929 to 1933 began before the stock market crash, economists generally agree that the stock market crash did not cause the Great Depression, but rather, made it worse than it otherwise would have been.

The then relatively new Federal Reserve System is viewed by many economists to have engaged in policies that actually led to the Great Depression. In the late 1920s, the Federal Reserve and President Hoover believed that the stock market boom of the time needed to be stopped because it was driven by speculation and was hurting the economy. Therefore, in 1928, the Fed engaged in extremely contractionary monetary policies by selling large amounts of bonds and by raising the discount rate. This had the desired effect of greatly reducing stock market prices in October 1929, but it had other unanticipated effects as well.

Because many people lost money in the stock market, consumption and investment fell. The unemployment rate rose from three percent in August 1929 to 25 percent in March 1933. Industrial production fell by close to 53 percent. The overall decline in the money supply was 35 percent, and prices fell by 33 percent. Moreover, a series of banking panics occurred, and a third of all banks closed or were taken over by others. Because there was no deposit insurance before the founding of the FDIC in 1933, depositors lost their money when banks failed, leading to a greater decline in consumption.

Most economists would agree that the Fed did not do enough to fight the Great Depression once it started. For one thing, the Fed did not serve well in its role as lender of last resort. Nobel laureate Milton Friedman and his co-author Anna Schwartz refer to the decrease in the money supply in the 1930s as the "great contraction." The contraction of the money supply led to deflation and declining production. With hindsight, many economists today believe that the Fed should have aggressively increased the money supply and provided liquidity to banks to stop the bank panics and bank failures. Although still a matter of debate, the failure of Fed policies provides one explanation of why the Great Depression was so severe from 1929 to 1933.

The Stock Market Crash of 1987

On Monday October 19, 1987, stock prices fell by 22.6 percent, more than on any other day in the 20th century. This resulted in an estimated loss of $500 billion to investors in a single day, and markets around the world were affected. However, this crash did not cause long-term damage to the economy. By the end of 1987 stock prices were at the same level as they were a year before, and by 1989 they had recovered to their peak 1987 levels. Unlike 1929, this stock market crash was not followed by a depression or even by a recession.

The causes of the crash of 1987 are a matter of dispute and probably involved a combination of factors. Causes cited include inflationary fears, overvalued stocks, computer trading, trade deficits and government deficits, and panic selling. Some economists believe that Federal Reserve policies may have contributed to the crash because the Fed raised the discount rate in 1987. These economists believe that this was not necessary and that it may have led to the inflationary fears that caused people to sell their stock. In general, however, Fed polices are seen to have lessened the effects of the stock market crash by providing liquidity to banks and preventing declines in consumption and investment that could have led to a recession.

On October 20, 1987, the day after the stock market crash, the Fed made the following announcement: "The Federal Reserve System, consistent with its responsibilities as the nation's central bank, affirmed today its readiness to serve as a source of liquidity to support the financial and economic system." The Fed then used open market operations to decrease the federal funds rate and greatly increased bank reserves. With this influx of reserves, banks could then make loans to individuals and businesses that had lost money when stock prices fell. When stock prices went back up, people were able to pay back their loans.

The Financial Crisis of the Late 2000s

The financial crisis that began in 2007 is the worst financial crisis since the Great Depression. It is referred to as the Financial Crisis of the Late 2000s, the Global Financial Crisis, or simply the Financial Crisis. The crisis has its origins in the real estate market. After the recession of 2001, mortgage interest rates were relatively low and people thought housing prices would continue to rise.

Because of the high demand for real estate, many banks made risky subprime mortgages to home buyers who did not have good credit. A **subprime mortgage** is a loan to buy real estate, given to someone with a relatively low credit rating. Housing prices reached a peak in 2006 and began to spiral downward in 2007. The decline in real estate prices hurt homeowners, banks, and other institutions that had invested heavily in real estate. Because of large losses in real estate, banks cut back on lending to individuals and businesses. Stock prices fell as people worried about the economy.

Many large companies that had invested heavily in real estate collapsed, including Bear Stearns, Lehman Brothers, and American International Group (AIG). The Fed stepped in to keep Bear Stearns out of bankruptcy, but Lehman Brothers was allowed to fail. The Fed also helped bail out AIG, a multinational insurance giant. The rationale for the bailouts was that preventing key large companies and banks from failing would lessen the negative effects of the crisis. Nonetheless, the crisis spread from the United States around the world, resulting in many bank failures in other countries and causing several countries, including Iceland and Pakistan, to apply for emergency assistance from the International Monetary Fund.

In December 2008 the NBER announced that the United States had been in recession since January 2008. This recession officially lasted until June 2009 and was one of the longest in recent history. However, even after the recession was officially over, unemployment remained very high and economic growth remained very sluggish. Political concerns about the government deficit made many members of Congress hesitant to support increased government spending, putting more pressure on the Fed to address the crisis.

Traditional expansionary monetary policy tools that reduce interest rates had already decreased the federal funds rate to record low levels. The Fed decreased the federal funds target from 5.25 percent in September 2007 to rates between 0 and .25 percent in December 2008, and later announced that it would maintain this low rate through 2013. Because traditional monetary policy could not lower short-term interest rates any further, the Fed turned to new and non-traditional tools to try to help the ailing economy. The new policies were designed to provide increased liquidity to banks and to provide other support for financial institutions that were in trouble. However, banks held much of the increased liquidity in the form of excess reserves rather than taking on risks from making loans.

One of the non-traditional policies that the Fed undertook to address the financial crisis is called quantitative easing (QE). **Quantitative easing** takes place when a central bank makes a large-scale purchase of assets to increase reserves in banks. The assets that the Fed purchased to deal with the crisis included mortgage-backed securities and Treasury securities. By purchasing long termed Treasury securities, the Fed hoped to keep longer-term interest rates low. When the Fed makes a large purchase of these securities, their price increases and their interest rate falls. The decrease in long-term interest rates should stimulate investment spending, create new jobs, and decrease unemployment. As of late 2011, the Fed had engaged in two rounds of QE. In the first round, the Fed purchased over $1 trillion worth of mortgage-backed securities to try to increase mortgage lending and help the ailing housing market. In the second round, the Fed purchased $600 billion of long-term Treasury securities to decrease long-term interest rates with the intent of increasing consumption and investment.

It is too early to evaluate the effects of Fed policies in dealing with the Financial Crisis of the late 2000s. The role of government and Fed oversight and regulation of financial markets in the crisis are also matters of debate. Supporters of Fed policies point to the extraordinary efforts that the Fed has made to address the problems of the crisis. Critics of Fed policies point to the long-run inflationary pressures that could result from these policies. One potential problem is that banks were holding massive amounts of excess reserves in late 2011, and a decision to lend out these reserves would cause the money supply to increase dramatically, leading to upward pressure on prices. The Fed is aware of this possibility and can use interest on reserves and other monetary policy tools to address this problem when the time comes. If the Fed increases the IOR rate above the rate banks could earn on loans, banks would have incentives to keep the reserves and not loan them out, thereby helping to avert inflation.

SUMMARY

The Federal Reserve System, the central bank in the United States, plays an important role in the economy. Established in 1913 to serve as a lender of last resort to commercial banks, the role and functions of the Fed have expanded over time. The most important function of the Fed today is to conduct monetary policy to promote price stability and maximum possible economic growth and employment. Open market operations are the main tool of traditional monetary policy, in absence of the financial crisis of the late 2000s. Open market operations occur when the Fed buys and sells government securities in the open bond market to affect bank reserves, the money supply, and interest rates. Although the Fed was created by an act of Congress, it is relatively independent of government control. This independence is to ensure that the conduct of monetary policy is free from political influence.

Although the Fed was created to prevent financial crises, it has not been completely successful in preventing them. As a relatively new organization during the Great Depression, the Fed is seen by many economists to have undertaken policies that actually worsened the depression. In contrast, Fed policies addressing the stock market crash of 1987 are generally seen to have prevented the crisis from having serious long-term effects. The Fed has added new tools to its traditional monetary policy tools to address the problems associated with the financial crises of the late 2000s. It is too early to evaluate the effects of these strategies.

Further Reading

About the Fed. Federal Reserve Bank of San Francisco. Retrieved online August 2011 at http://www.frbsf.org/federalreserve/.

Carlstrom, Charles T., and Timothy S. Fuerst. Monetary Policy in a World with Interest on Reserves. Federal Reserve Bank of Cleveland. 2010. Retrieved online September 2011 at http://www.clevelandfed.org/research/commentary/2010/2010-4.cfm.

Cowen, David. "The First Bank of the United States." *EH.net Encyclopedia.* Retrieved online August 2011 at http://eh.net/encyclopedia/article/cowen.banking.first_bank .us.

"Economic Crisis and Market Upheavals." *New York Times Topics.* Retrieved online September 2011 at http://topics.nytimes.com/top/reference/timestopics/subjects/c/ credit_crisis/index.html?scp=1&sq=economic%20crisis%20&st=cse.

FDIC: Who is the FDIC? Retrieved online August 2011 at http://www.fdic.gov/about/learn/ symbol/index.html.

Federal Reserve Discount Window. Retrieved online August 2011 at http://www.frb discountwindow.org/index.cfm.

"Lessons from History: Stock Market Crashes." *Learning, Earning and Investing.* New York: National Council on Economic Education, 2004.

Monetary Policy. Board of Governors of the Federal Reserve System. Retrieved online August 2011 at http://www.federalreserve.gov/.

National Park Service. The U.S. Constitution: Second Bank of the United States. Retrieved online August 2011 at http://www.cr.nps.gov/history/online_books/butowsky2/ constitution7.htm

Parker, Randall. "An Overview of the Great Depression." Posted 2.5.2010 on EH.net. Retrieved online September 2011 at http://eh.net/encyclopedia/article/parker. depression.

"Quantitative Easing Explained." *Liber8: Economic Information Newsletter.* April 2011. Federal Reserve Bank of St. Louis. Retrieved online September 2011 at http://liber8 .stlouisfed.org/newsletter/2011/201104.pdf.

Timberlake, Richard H. "The Original Federal Reserve System." *The Concise Encyclopedia of Economics.* Retrieved online August 2011 at http://www.econlib.org/library/Enc/ FederalReserveSystem.html.

CHAPTER 9

MACROECONOMIC SCHOOLS OF THOUGHT AND DISPUTES IN MACROECONOMICS

Harry Truman, the 33rd President of the United States, once said "Give me a one-handed economist! All my economists say 'on one hand . . . on the other hand.'" Economists are not always able to agree on what to do to improve the economy. And as President Truman's comment implies, making decisions about economic issues is not entirely cut and dry. Solutions to macroeconomic problems such as unemployment and inflation are complicated. Even the most famous economists, educated at the best schools and working on important jobs at prestigious institutions, frequently disagree about what is the best course of action. This lack of consensus occurs in part because there are many things about macroeconomics that we simply do not know. The economy comprises millions of people making independent decisions, and events and interactions are constantly changing. The lack of consensus also stems from different opinions about how the economy works. These different opinions are sometimes influenced by, and spill over to, the political arena.

This chapter investigates some of the major economic schools of thought and alternative viewpoints on how the economy works. It includes an overview of several economic theories (classical, Keynesian, monetarist, supply-side, and rational expectations) and then looks at some current macroeconomic disputes. A number of these disputes center on whether we take a long-run or a short-run perspective of the economy, while other disputes relate to whether the government should take an active or passive role in trying to solve problems in the economy.

AN OVERVIEW OF MACROECONOMIC SCHOOLS OF THOUGHT
The Classical Economists

The classical school of thought in economics refers to the philosophies of many of the economic thinkers of the Western world between 1776 and the Great Depression. It began with the ideas of Scottish philosopher Adam Smith in a book formally titled *An Inquiry into the Nature and Causes of the Wealth of Nations*. More commonly known as *The Wealth of Nations*, the book was published in 1776, during the first century of the Industrial Revolution that began in Great Britain. Smith's observations and ideas provide the basis of the classical school of thought and the foundations of modern capitalism. Other classical economists include Jean Baptiste Say of France and British political philosophers David Ricardo, Thomas Malthus, and John Stuart Mill. The term neoclassical economics is used to refer to the ideas of economists from the 1870s to the 1930s who emphasized marginal analysis and mathematics, including Alfred Marshall, William Stanley Jevons and Irving Fisher. However, the term neoclassical economics is also used to refer to mainstream economic theory today.

Although the ideas of the individual classical economists differed in theoretical emphasis, we can identify some common themes. For example, the classical economists focused on the long-run. In macroeconomics, the **long run** is the time period when all prices are flexible, so there are no overall surpluses or shortages. The classical school of thought emphasizes that when wages, prices, and interest rates are flexible and adjust by supply and demand, the economy is self-correcting. Problems such as unemployment are thus solved without the government taking action. The logic behind this was that unemployment would cause wages to fall because some unemployed workers would be willing to work for less than the going wage in order to have a job. Responding to falling wages, businesses would be willing and able to hire more workers, which would reduce unemployment.

Classical economic theory implies that with flexible prices, situations like the Great Depression—when there was not enough demand to purchase the

Classical School of Thought

- Economy is self-correcting
- No long-run unemployment (flexible wages)
- Aggregate Demand = Aggregate Supply (Say's Law)
- No general oversupply of goods (flexible prices)
- Savings = Investment (flexible interest rates)
- Laissez-faire role for government

goods and services available at full employment—could not occur. According to **Say's Law**, named after Jean Baptiste Say, supply creates its own demand. The idea behind Say's Law is that you go to work to supply something because you demand something of equal value. For example, if you supply $1,000 worth of apples, it is because you either demand those apples or something else worth $1,000. Otherwise, you would not work to supply the apples. So in the aggregate, the amount supplied in the economy will be equal to the amount demanded. There may be shortages of some things and surpluses of others, and the prices and quantities of these goods will adjust accordingly. But overall, aggregate demand will equal aggregate supply, and there will be no general oversupply of goods.

Will Say's Law still hold if people want to save? For example, what if you decided to save some of your $1,000 from producing apples, rather than buying $1,000 worth of goods and services right away? According to classical theory, this would not be a problem because interest rates will adjust so that savings will equal investment. If savings increase, interest rates will fall and this will encourage businesses to borrow more for investment purposes. Therefore aggregate demand will still equal aggregate supply when taking savings into account.

Since the classical economists believed that problems in the economy correct themselves, they believed in a limited role for government in the economy. They advocated a **laissez-faire** role for government. This French expression means "to let things happen on their own." When applied to the role of government, laissez-faire means that the government should not interfere with the economy.

The Keynesians

John Maynard Keynes was a British economist who wrote the book *The General Theory of Employment, Interest and Money*, often called *The General Theory*. The book was published in 1936, during the Great Depression. The Great Depression was a severe worldwide economic downturn affecting production and employment. During the Great Depression, the U.S. unemployment rate rose to 25 percent of the labor force, and real GDP fell by 25 percent. Keynes had studied economics at Cambridge University under neoclassical economist Alfred Marshall and was well schooled in classical economics theory. Nonetheless he believed that the long-run focus of classical theory, which was to wait for the economy to correct itself and reach full employment on its own, was not the best way to deal with a situation like the Great Depression. In a now famous quote Keynes observed, "The long run is a misleading guide to current affairs. In the long run we are all dead." Keynes believed that it was the responsibility of government to intervene in the economy if there were problems.

Keynesian theory was at the forefront of economic policy from the Great Depression through the 1960s and has been called "the Keynesian revolution."

Keynesian School of Thought

- Persistent unemployment may exist.
- Wages and prices are sticky.
- There can be insufficient aggregate demand.
- Interest rates do not equate savings and investment.
- The government should intervene to help the economy in periods of instability.
- Policies should address aggregate demand.

Keynesians take a short-run focus and point out that wages and prices are not always flexible. Wages, they contend, are especially "sticky" and slow to fall when there is unemployment. This wage stickiness means that unemployment may persist and not go away on its own. When many people are unemployed, there is not enough aggregate demand in the economy to buy the goods and services that would be produced if there were full employment. Therefore the government should implement policies to increase aggregate demand. Keynesians do not believe that supply creates its own demand; it is demand that leads to supply.

Planned investment spending, which includes the amount businesses plan to spend on capital goods and construction, is part of aggregate demand. Keynes believed that investment spending was very volatile and caused unexpected changes in aggregate demand. He did not believe that flexible interest rates would ensure that all savings would be borrowed for investment purposes, because savings were primarily a function of income and not interest rates. When aggregate demand from the private sector is insufficient to guarantee full employment, the government and central bank should step in to increase aggregate demand.

Keynesians believe that during a recession or depression, the government should engage in the expansionary fiscal policies of increasing government spending or decreasing taxes to increase aggregate demand. The central bank could also engage in expansionary monetary policies to increase the money supply, decrease interest rates, and increase investment spending. Keynesians generally prefer fiscal policies over monetary policies because they believe fiscal policies work more quickly and are more effective in affecting aggregate demand. In times of inflation, the government and central bank should engage in contractionary policies.

The Monetarists

There were always critics of Keynes and his followers, but it was the monetarists, led by Nobel Laureate Milton Friedman, who ushered in what has

Monetarist School of Thought

- "Money matters most."
- MV = PQ
- Emphasis on real versus nominal values
- Active policies cause macroeconomic instability
- Monetary rules are preferred to discretionary policies

been called a "monetarist counterrevolution" in macroeconomic theory in the late 1960s. The phrase "money matters most" captures the essence of the monetarists' views. The monetarists believe that the money supply is the most important macroeconomic variable in determining stability and growth in the economy.

The **equation of exchange**, MV = PQ, can be used to demonstrate the importance of the quantity of money in the economy. This equation was developed by Irving Fisher of Yale University (and a similar version was developed by Alfred Marshall at Cambridge) in the early 1900s. The equation of exchange is an early formulation of monetarism because it shows the importance of the quantity of money. In the equation, M stands for the money supply, the quantity of money in the economy that is available for spending. V stands for the **velocity of money**, how many times a dollar is spent on average during a certain time period. P stands for the overall price level in the economy. Q stands for the quantity of goods and services produced.

Because the left-hand side of the equation of exchange represents total spending on goods and services and the right-hand side represents the value of the goods and services purchased, the equation is always true. It simply means that when money is spent, it is spent on something. Or that the value of everything that has been purchased is equal to the value of the money (times velocity)

Equation of Exchange: MV = PQ

M = Money supply
V = Velocity of money; how many times an average dollar is spent in a time period
P = Price level
Q = Quantity of goods and services

that was used to make the purchases. The Q in the equation can be viewed as real GDP, and P times Q can be viewed as nominal GDP.

Neoclassical economists believed that velocity was stable and constant. Monetarists believe that although not constant, velocity is relatively stable and predictable. Assume, for simplicity, that velocity is constant and that the economy has reached long-run full employment, so that Q is also constant. If the central bank increases the money supply, the equation shows that the price level P would have to rise. If velocity is fairly constant and the money supply grows faster than real output, this will cause an increase in P and will be inflationary.

Friedman conducted research on the effects of changes in the money supply on business cycles in U.S. history. This research led him to conclude that instability in the money supply leads to instability in the business cycle. Therefore monetarists prefer that central banks follow rules for changing the money supply, rather than using discretionary policies to try to "fine tune" the economy. One rule that monetarists have advocated is that the rate of growth of the money supply should be constant and predictable, and roughly equal to the potential growth rate of real GDP. More recently monetarists have been in favor of inflation targeting, which also limits central bank discretion. Because the money supply affects aggregate demand, monetarists, like Keynesians, put an emphasis on changes in aggregate demand to solve the economy's problems.

Supply-Side Economics

Although economists have always known that the supply of goods and services is important for employment and growth, the term supply-side economics is often associated with the 1980s and the presidency of Ronald Reagan. Reagan wanted to decrease the size of the government sector of the economy. Supply-side economists advocate implementing policies designed to provide incentives

Supply-Side Economics

- Emphasis is on increasing aggregate supply rather than aggregate demand.
- Decreasing taxes on businesses provides incentives to produce more.
- Decreasing taxes on individuals provides incentives to work more.
- Tax decreases will not lead to increased budget deficits.
- Associated with Ronald Reagan and desire to decrease size of government.

for private businesses to increase aggregate supply. This is the idea of supply-side fiscal policy discussed in Chapter 6.

Supply-side theorists believe that reducing taxes both on businesses and individuals is the way to provide incentives to increase aggregate supply in the private sector. If businesses pay lower taxes, they will have more after-tax income to use to invest in new capital and to expand. This will increase aggregate supply. If individuals have lower marginal tax rates, they will have incentives to work more. Your marginal tax rate is the percentage in taxes that you pay on your last (or next) dollar of taxable income. For example, if you worked an additional hour and 90 percent of your income went to taxes, your marginal tax rate would be 90 percent. In this case, you very well may decide that it is not worth working that extra hour. However, if your marginal tax rate were 10 percent, you would be more likely to decide to work that extra hour.

One of the criticisms of supply-side economics is that reducing taxes will make the budget deficit, and the national debt, worse. Supply-side economists argue that this is not true and that reducing tax rates can actually result in more tax revenue. For example, if decreasing taxes provided incentives for businesses to produce more and provided incentives to individuals to work more, aggregate supply would increase. This increase in supply would result in more taxable income to businesses and individuals. Even though the tax rates were lower, the government could end up collecting more overall tax revenue because of the increase in aggregate supply.

Rational Expectations

The rational expectations school of thought puts an emphasis on the importance of expectations to determine what happens in the economy. The theory was first developed by John F. Muth in the 1960s, although the importance of expectations was also recognized by many earlier economists. Rational expectations theory received widespread attention when it was adopted by Robert Lucas, Thomas Sargent, and others in the 1970s as part of the new classical school of thought. Lucas won the Nobel Prize in Economics in 1995; Sargent was awarded the Nobel Prize in Economics in 2011.

Rational expectations theory operates under the assumptions that people make rational decisions and that they are informed about fiscal and monetary policies and the outcomes of these policies. For example, if the Federal Reserve announced that it was increasing the money supply to lower interest rates, people would know that in the long run this would cause inflation. What would rational and informed people do if they expected inflation? If they were lenders, they would raise interest rates so they would be paid back the same amount of purchasing power that they lend out. These increased interest rates would offset the Fed's attempt to lower interest rates, rendering the Fed's expansionary monetary policy ineffective. In the extreme, rational expectations theory predicts

Rational Expectations

- Emphasis on importance of expectations.
- Assumptions that people are rational and informed.
- Active policies work only if people are fooled.
- In the long run, people correctly anticipate policy effects and offset them.

that changes that take place due to expectations would take place immediately after a policy was announced or anticipated.

The conclusion of the rational expectations school with respect to fiscal and monetary policies is that these policies work only if people are fooled. If the Fed were able to somehow trick people so they did not know about increases in the money supply, then people would not anticipate inflation and would not raise interest rates. But people cannot be systematically fooled by policy makers, so eventually they come to correctly anticipate fiscal and monetary policies. Therefore, in the long run, active policies do not achieve their desired outcomes.

The Mainstream View

There are many schools of thought in addition to those discussed above, including the Austrian school, behavioral economics, real business cycle theory, Marxism, and new Keynesianism. And there are divisions within the schools that we have discussed. In general, economists today do not identify solely with one school of thought and ignore the contributions of other economic thinkers. Most economists identify with a mainstream view of economics that borrows from all of the major schools of thought.

Although there are variations of what is considered mainstream, most would agree that in the long run, the economy could reach full employment equilibrium on its own, but how long this would take is a matter of debate. Most agree that wages and prices are sticky in the short run. This calls for some government and central bank intervention, although what kind of intervention and how much is disputed. The importance of the money supply is widely recognized among mainstream economists, as is the finding that velocity is not stable. The importance of supply-side factors is not disputed. There is widespread agreement about the importance of expectations, but not about the instantaneous adjustment of macroeconomic variables to expectations.

DISPUTES IN MACROECONOMICS

Macroeconomics is not an exact science, so there are always discussions and debates about what is best for the economy. Some of the disputes are about the economic effects of specific programs related to such things as health care or immigration. And some of the disputes are over broad issues such as the proper time frame for viewing economic decisions and the role of government in the economy. This section investigates some of these broader-based areas where macroeconomists disagree.

Long-Run Versus Short-Run Focus

One issue that economists disagree on is the proper time frame for viewing how the economy works. Some believe that the long-run perspective is best, while others counter that the short-run view is best. Because of the way "long-run" is defined in macroeconomics, most are likely to agree that there would be full employment in the long run. However, there is no agreement on how long it will take for this to occur if prices, wages, and interest rates are sticky instead of flexible.

The classical economists took a long-run focus, and this is also the perspective of the monetarists and rational expectations theorists. From this viewpoint, the economy will reach equilibrium on its own so the role of government in the economy is limited. If, on the other hand, the short run is the proper time frame for viewing how the economy works, there can be surpluses of labor causing unemployment and surpluses of goods and services leading to lower production in the future. From the short-run perspective, the government and central bank should intervene to try to help the economy.

Active Versus Passive Role for Government and the Central Bank

The proper role for government and the central bank in stabilizing the economy is related to the long-run versus short-run issue. If the economy is experiencing problems but you believe that it will quickly reach full employment equilibrium on its own, then you may not be in favor of active, discretionary fiscal and monetary policies. If, however, you believe that the economy will be stuck with its problems for a long time, then you may be in favor of active, discretionary fiscal and monetary policies.

Some economists believe that it would be better if the government and central bank followed policy rules rather than engaging in discretionary policies. They argue that discretionary policies can be destabilizing and cause more problems than they solve. Both fiscal and monetary policies have unpredictable lags. The lags can result in situations where by the time a policy takes effect, things may have changed, making the policy inappropriate or counterproductive. For example, if an expansionary fiscal or monetary policy designed to get the economy out of a recession took effect after the economy had recovered and was near the peak of the business cycle, the lag could lead to inflation. And if contractionary policies designed to decrease inflation did not take effect until the economy had entered a recession, these policies could make the recession worse.

Monetary Policy Rules

As explained earlier in this chapter, monetarists advocated a monetary policy rule where the money supply would grow at a rate consistent with the potential rate of growth of real GDP. This would take away the Fed's discretion to increase and decrease the money supply at will. Inflation targeting is another type of monetary policy rule, where the central bank must keep inflation at a certain level or within a certain range. And the Taylor Rule is a rule of thumb that tells the Fed how to set the federal funds rate. It assumes that the Fed has a target rate of inflation of two percent. If GDP is equal to its potential level and inflation is two percent, the rule stipulates that the federal funds target rate should be four percent. For every one percent that GDP is below its potential, the Fed should decrease the federal funds rate by one-half percent. For every one percent that inflation is below the target rate of two percent, the Fed should also decrease the federal funds rate by one-half percent. The rule is reversed if GDP is above its potential and inflation is above two percent.

Fiscal Policy Rule: Balancing the Budget

There are also fiscal policy rules that would constrain the ability of the government to conduct discretionary fiscal policy. One proposed fiscal policy rule is that the government should be required to balance its budget annually. There are frequently calls in Congress for a balanced budget amendment to the Constitution. This would take away the discretion of the federal government to spend more than it collects in revenues in any fiscal year.

Although there is widespread agreement that unconstrained government spending is problematic, requiring the government to balance its budget every year could create problems of its own. Requiring a balanced budget every year, for example, would mean that the government could not maintain any annual deficits or surpluses. Consider what would happen during recessions when government tax receipts fall because incomes fall. If the government could never have a deficit, government spending would have to fall as well, which could make the recession worse. By the same token, if the government could never have a budget surplus, this balanced-budget policy could fuel inflation. At the peak of the business cycle, when inflation is a potential problem, government tax receipts are high because unemployment is low and incomes are high. If surpluses were not allowed, the government would have to spend all of the revenues, a move which could itself be inflationary. For these reasons, mainstream economists are not in favor of requiring annually balanced budgets.

Mainstream View of Rules versus Discretion

Mainstream economists generally recognize the need for some discretionary policies rather than strict adherence to rules. For the most part, modern-day recessions have been less frequent and less severe than those of the past, and discretionary policies are credited with helping to achieve this result. Fed policies are credited with helping to reduce inflation in the early 1980s and for reducing the severity of the financial crisis that began in 2007. While recognizing that there are problems associated with large budget deficits and uncontrolled spending, the mainstream view is that the problems of business cycles would be worse without discretionary fiscal and monetary policies.

SUMMARY

There are no easy answers to the economy's problems. There are several different schools of thought about how the economy operates, and these different perspectives lead to differences of opinion about what is best for the economy and what is the proper role of government. Some of the major schools of thought are the classical, Keynesian, monetarist, supply-side, and rational expectations points of view. The mainstream viewpoint recognizes contributions from the major schools of thought and seeks to recommend policies and approaches that will address different situations. From a long-run perspective, if the economy adjusts to full-employment equilibrium on its own, then active discretionary policies are not necessary. From a short-run perspective, active discretionary policies may help to reduce the severity of problems associated with business cycles. Although there is much that we do not know about macroeconomics, knowledge gained from past experiences will help to address problems that arise in the future.

Further Reading

Henderson, David R. ed. *The Concise Encyclopedia of Economics. Library of Economics and Liberty.* Retrieved online March 2012 at http://www.econlib.org/library/CEE .html.

Keynes, John Maynard. *The General Theory of Employment, Interest, and Money.* First published 1936. Retrieved online March 2012 at http://ebooks.adelaide.edu.au/k/ keynes/john_maynard/k44g/

Shim, Jae K., and Joel G. Siegel. *Dictionary of Economics.* New York: John Wiley and Sons, 1995.

Smith, Adam. *An Inquiry into the Nature and Causes of the Wealth of Nations.* First published 1776. Retrieved online March 2012 at http://www.econlib.org/library/Smith/ smWN.html

aggregate   A whole or total amount of something, such as aggregate demand or aggregate supply.

aggregate demand   The total amount of goods and services that will be purchased at different price levels in an economy.

aggregate supply   The total amount of goods and services that will be produced at different price levels.

allocative efficiency   Occurs when the goods and services that are produced are those that people value and are willing to buy. This means that economic resources (land, labor, capital, and entrepreneurship) are allocated to the production of the goods people want.

automatic stabilizers   Changes in taxes and government spending that take place due to already existing legislation. Also called built-in stabilizers and non-discretionary fiscal policy.

balanced budget   With respect to the federal government budget, means that government revenues are equal to government expenditures in any given fiscal year.

bank panics   A type of financial crisis that occurs when depositors are worried that their bank will fail and hurry to withdraw their deposits in the form of cash. Also called runs on banks.

barter   Trading goods and services without money; exchanging goods and services for each other.

base year   A year that is used to compare how much prices have changed over time.

bond   A financial instrument representing debt to the issuer; a type of IOU.

budget deficit   With respect to the federal government, occurs if the government spends more than it receives in revenue in any fiscal year.

budget surplus   With respect to the federal government, occurs if the government receives more in revenue than it spends in any fiscal year.

business cycle   The periodic ups and downs in the level of economic activity in an economy. Usually divided into four phases: expansion, peak, contraction or recession, and trough.

capital   As an economic resource, goods that are used to produce other goods and do not get used up in the production process.

centralized decision making   When decisions are made by a few people in power rather than by many private individuals.

COLA   Cost of living adjustment; an adjustment in earnings to offset a loss of purchasing power due to inflation.

command economic system   An economic system in which questions of what to produce, how to produce, and for whom to produce are answered by those in power.

commercial bank   An all-purpose bank that offers a variety of services such as checking accounts, time and savings accounts, business loans, and mortgage loans.

commodity money   Money that has intrinsic value (such as gold or silver).

Consumer Price Index (CPI)   The most commonly used measure of inflation in the United States. Computed monthly by the Bureau of Labor Statistics, it measures price changes for a collection of goods and services that are representative of what a typical urban consumer might buy.

contractionary fiscal policy   When the government decreases its spending or increases taxes in order to decrease aggregate demand. Intended to address inflation or potential inflation.

contractionary monetary policy   When the Fed decreases the money supply to raise interest rates to decrease aggregate demand. Intended to address inflation or potential inflation.

core inflation rate   A measure of inflation that does not include changes in the prices of food and energy.

cost-push inflation   Inflation that occurs when business costs increase and businesses pass on the cost increases to consumers in the form of higher prices.

counterfeit money   Money that has been produced illegally.

credit union   A type of thrift institution that requires membership. Credit unions often charge members lower interest on loans and pay higher interest on savings than other types of banks.

crowding out   When increases in government spending financed through borrowing result in increases in interest rates and reductions in private spending.

currency   Paper money and coins.

cyclical deficits   Government budget deficits that occur due to the business cycle.

cyclical unemployment   The unemployment that occurs as a result of the downward phase of the business cycle. When the economy is declining and in a contraction, cyclical unemployment increases.

decision lag   The amount of time it takes for policy makers to agree on what to do about a problem in the economy.

deflation   A sustained decrease in the overall price level.

demand deposit   A checking account from which you can withdraw your money whenever you want to (on demand) without penalty. There are no restrictions on how many checks you can write or how much you can withdraw.

demand shocks   Unexpected, sudden changes in aggregate demand.

demand-pull inflation   Inflation that occurs when spending or demand increases faster than output or supply; too much money chasing too few goods and services.

depreciation   Occurs when capital goods wear out over time. Also called "consumption of fixed capital" in the national income and product accounts.

depression   A severe recession.

discount rate   The interest rate that the Fed charges to banks and thrift institutions when they borrow from the Fed.

discouraged workers   Those who would like to work but have given up looking for jobs because they do not think there is a chance that they will find a job.

discretionary fiscal policy   When the government deliberately decides to change taxes or spending to deal with a certain situation, such as a recession or inflation.

disposable personal income   Personal income minus current personal taxes; how much income you have to spend or save after you have paid your taxes.

durable goods   In the Bureau of Economic Analysis GDP accounts, goods that will last for three or more years with normal usage. Examples are washing machines and cars.

econometrics   The field of economics that applies statistics and mathematics to economic models.

economic equity   The quality of being just or fair with respect to the economy. Because different people have different opinions about what is fair and what is not, it is not easy to judge whether this goal is being met.

economic freedom   On an individual level, refers to the right to make your own choices about such things as what to consume, what to produce, what education to pursue, what career to pursue, and whether to start your own business or work for someone else.

economic growth   Occurs when more goods and services are produced in one time period than before. Economic growth is usually measured by increases in real GDP, or real GDP per capita.

economic resources   The natural resources, labor, capital and entrepreneurial resources necessary to produce goods and services. Economic resources are also called resources, productive resources, factors of production, factors, or inputs.

economic stability   An economy that does not fluctuate widely. A stable economy is characterized by steady economic growth, employment, and prices.

economic system   The way an economy organizes the ownership, production, and distribution of its economic resources.

economics   A social science concerned with how societies choose to use their scarce resources to satisfy people's wants.

economy   The consumption, production, and distribution of goods and services in a certain area, such as a country.

effect lag   The amount of time it takes for a policy to affect output, employment, or prices in the economy.

electronic money (e-money)   Money that is transferred electronically from a buyer's account to a seller's account.

employed   According to the Bureau of Labor Statistics, someone who did any work for pay or profit during the past week, or who worked 15 or more hours of unpaid work in a family business, or was temporarily absent from a regular job.

entrepreneurship   The economic resource that organizes the other factors of production and undertakes risk with the goal of making a profit. Entrepreneurs often have new ideas and start new businesses.

equation of exchange (MV = PQ)   The tautology that says that the money supply times the velocity of money is equal to the price level times the quantity of real output.

excess reserves   The amount of reserves that a bank holds in addition to the required reserves.

excise taxes   Taxes on the sale or consumption of goods, such as gasoline or tobacco.

expansionary fiscal policy   When the government either increases its spending or decreases taxes in order to increase aggregate demand, production, and employment. Intended to address recessions or other periods of high unemployment and declining or sluggish economic growth.

expansionary monetary policy   When the Fed increases the money supply and lowers interest rates to increase aggregate demand, production, and employment. Intended to address recessions or other periods of high unemployment and declining or sluggish economic growth.

exports   Goods and services produced in one country and sold to buyers in foreign countries. (For the United States, goods and services produced in the United States that are sold to buyers in other countries.)

federal funds rate   The interest rate that banks charge each other for overnight loans.

fiat money   Money that the government declares is money. It is not convertible into a fixed amount of gold, silver, or other assets.

final goods and services   A good or service consumed by the buyer or the end user. (Contrast to an intermediate good.)

financial intermediary   An institution such as a bank that receives deposits from savers and lends the funds to borrowers.

fiscal policy   When the government changes spending and taxes to try to stabilize the economy.

fiscal year   A one-year period for budget or accounting purposes. The government has a budget for every fiscal year. The U.S. government's fiscal year runs from October 1 to September 30.

Fisher Effect   The tendency for nominal interest rates to be affected by expected inflation; nominal interest rates are equal to real interest rates plus the expected inflation rate.

fractional reserve system of banking   A system where banks do not have to keep 100 percent of their deposits in reserve.

frictional unemployment   Unemployment that occurs when workers are between jobs, such as when they voluntarily quit one job to look for another job, or when they look for their first job. It is sometimes called "search unemployment" because people are searching for a new job or a better job.

gross domestic product (GDP)   The total amount of final goods and services produced in an economy in a certain time period.

Gross Domestic Product Deflator (GDP deflator)   A measure of price changes found by dividing nominal GDP by real GDP, and multiplying by 100.

gross domestic product (GDP) price index   A measure of price changes that comprises spending on the goods and services in GDP, including prices paid in consumption, investment, government consumption, and net exports.

gross national product (GNP)   The market value of final goods and services produced by the residents of a country, either within the country or in another country.

human capital   The knowledge, skills, and training that people acquire in schools or on the job. As you acquire education, training, or job experience, you are investing in human capital.

hyperinflation   When the price level rises very rapidly and there is a very high rate of inflation.

imports   Goods or services produced in a foreign country that are purchased by buyers in the domestic country. (For the United States, goods and services produced in other countries that are purchased by people in the United States.)

incentive   Something that encourages people to act in a certain way.

inflation   A sustained increase in the overall price level.

institution   An organization, custom, or system of beliefs that is devoted to promoting a specific cause.

intermediate goods   Items used in the production process of a final good or service. For example, a windshield is an intermediate good in the production of a car.

inventories   The stock of goods that have been produced but that have not been sold.

investment   In macroeconomics, spending by businesses on capital goods.

labor   As an economic resource, the work of humans in the production of goods and services. Labor results from both physical and mental skills and talents.

labor force   The civilian labor force is the part of the population that is 16 years old or older, not on active duty in the Armed Forces, not institutionalized, and is either working or looking for work.

labor force participation rate The percentage of the working-age population that is working or looking for work and is therefore in the labor force.

labor productivity The output that results per hour that people work. Also called worker productivity.

laissez-faire To let things happen on their own. When applied to the role of government, laissez-faire means that the government should leave the economy alone.

land As an economic resource, all natural resources or gifts of nature including land, trees, oil, wind power, and so on.

leading indicator A measure of economic performance that tends to go up or down before the economy as a whole does.

lender of last resort The role the central bank performs when it lends money to financial institutions when no one else is willing or able to do so.

liquidity The ease of converting something into cash.

long run In macroeconomics, the time period when all prices are flexible. All markets clear in the aggregate and there are no surpluses or shortages.

macroeconomics The study of economic decision making for the whole economy or for major sectors of the economy. Macroeconomics addresses topics such as GDP, unemployment, and inflation.

marginal propensity to consume (MPC) The percentage of a change in income that is consumed.

marginal propensity to save (MPS) The percentage of a change in income that is saved.

marginal tax rate The percentage in taxes paid on the last dollar of taxable income earned.

market Anywhere something is bought or sold.

market economic system An economic system where the questions of what, how, and for whom are answered by individual consumers and producers through markets.

market value The prices for which goods and services are sold in the marketplace.

medium of exchange The function of money that makes trading easier because money is a generally accepted form of payment for goods and services.

microeconomics The study of economic decision making by individuals, business firms, and industries. Microeconomics addresses topics such as how prices are determined for specific products and decision making by businesses to maximize profits.

ministries   In the former Soviet Union, governmental organizations in charge of different industries such as steel, agriculture, and machinery.

mixed economic system   An economic system that contains some characteristics of command economic systems, some characteristics of traditional economic systems, and some characteristics of market economic systems. In practice, all economic systems are mixed.

M1   The measure of the money supply that consists primarily of currency in circulation and checking-type deposits.

monetary policy   When the central bank changes the money supply and interest rates to achieve national goals.

money   Anything that is generally accepted in payment for goods and services, or in the repayment of debts.

money market mutual fund   A type of savings account that pools the savings of many people and invests in short-term debt securities such as Treasury bills and pay interest to the savers.

money multiplier   How much money can be created from excess reserves. If excess reserves of $1,000 lead to increases in the money supply of $2,000, the money multiplier is 2. Also called the deposit expansion multiplier.

M2   The measure of the money supply that includes M1 plus deposits in small (under $100,000) savings-type accounts.

multiplier   A change in an economic variable that brings about greater changes in another variable. For example, the expenditure multiplier is the idea that any change in spending can have a greater effect on output (GDP) and income.

national debt   The total of all of the annual budget deficits, minus any annual budget surpluses, of the federal government over time. Also called the public debt, the federal government debt, and the U.S. government debt.

national income   The sum of rent, wages and salaries, interest, and profits, and also including taxes on production and imports.

natural rate of unemployment   The rate of unemployment that would exist if there were only frictional and structural unemployment, but no cyclical unemployment.

net domestic product (NDP)   Gross domestic product minus depreciation (consumption of fixed capital).

net national product (NNP)   Gross national product minus depreciation (consumption of fixed capital).

nominal values   Values measured in current prices. For example, nominal GDP for the year 2010 is GDP valued at prices in existence in 2010.

non-durable goods   In the Bureau of Economic Analysis GDP accounts , goods that wear out in less than three years with normal usage. Examples are food and clothing.

Okun's Law (or Okun's rule of thumb)   The observation that for every one percent increase in unemployment above the natural rate, GDP will decrease by two percent below its potential.

open market operations   The purchase and sale of U.S. government securities by the Federal Reserve System.

opportunity cost   What is given up when you have to make a choice; the next best use of scarce resources.

payroll tax   The tax that an employer is required to withhold from your paycheck. Examples of payroll taxes are the withholding for Social Security and Medicare.

per capita   Per person. For example, GDP per capita is computed by taking the total amount of GDP in a country and dividing this by the number of people in the country.

personal income   The income people receive from all sources.

potential GDP   The level of GDP that would exist if there were full employment in the economy.

production possibilities model   A model that shows the possible combinations of two goods (or two categories of goods) that could be produced with a given amount of resources.

productive efficiency   Producing goods and services at the lowest cost possible and not wasting resources.

productivity   The amount of output that results from a unit of input in a certain time period, such as an hour.

proprietors   People who own their own businesses.

quantitative easing   When a central bank makes a large scale purchase of assets to increase reserves in banks.

real GDP   GDP that has been adjusted for changes in overall prices using a base year.

real rate of interest   The interest rate that would exist if there were no inflation.

real values   Values that have been adjusted for changes in overall prices.

recession   A significant decline in economic activity throughout the economy, lasting more than a few months. Usually affects real GDP, real income, employment, production, and sales.

recognition lag   The length of time between when a problem occurs in the economy and when policy makers realize that it has occurred.

representative money   Something circulating as money that is backed (or represents) a certain amount of a commodity such as gold or silver.

reserve currency   A foreign currency held by financial institutions and central banks, which can be used to pay off international debts. The U.S. dollar is the major reserve currency in the world today.

reserve requirement   The amount that banks have to keep in reserve to back up checking-type deposits. This is set by the Federal Reserve. Also called the reserve ratio since it is expressed as a percentage of checkable deposits.

rule of 72   Tells approximately how long it will take something to double, by dividing 72 by a rate of change. For example, if GDP is growing at a rate of four percent per year, it will double in about 18 years (72/4 = 18).

Say's Law   Supply creates its own demand. In the aggregate, this implies that there will be no overall shortages or surpluses in the economy.

scarcity   The situation that occurs because there are not enough resources in the world to satisfy peoples' wants.

seasonal unemployment   Unemployment that occurs due to seasonal or recurring changes in available jobs or in the labor supply.

short run   In macroeconomics, the time period when all markets have not adjusted to their equilibrium levels because wages or other input prices are not totally flexible.

specialization   When people produce one or a few goods and services, rather than producing everything for themselves.

stabilization policies   Policies that attempt to smooth out the problems of inflation and unemployment associated with the peak and trough of the business cycle. Fiscal policy also tries to keep GDP growing at its potential rate, and to keep actual GDP close to potential GDP.

standard of living   How well off people are in terms of the goods and services they have, as well as other measures of well-being such as life expectancy and access to education and health care.

store of value   The function that money performs when you get paid in money today and can save it to spend at a later date.

structural deficits   Federal government budget deficits occurring from discretionary fiscal policy.

structural unemployment   Unemployment that occurs when workers are not hired because they do not have the right skills for the jobs that are available.

subprime mortgage   A loan to buy real estate given to someone with a relatively low credit rating.

supply shocks   Unexpected, sudden changes in aggregate supply.

supply side fiscal policy   Fiscal policy that focuses on reducing marginal tax rates to provide incentives to workers and businesses, which will result in increases in production and aggregate supply.

thrifts (thrift institutions)   Credit unions, savings banks, and savings and loan banks. Today these institutions perform many of the same functions as commercial banks but are more likely to specialize in time deposits and mortgages.

time deposit   A type of savings account that pays interest for a certain period of time, such as one year or three years.

trade deficit   When the value of a country's imports is greater than the value of its exports. The United States has had a trade deficit every year since the mid 1970s.

trade-off   The exchange of one thing for another.

traditional economic system   An economic system where decisions about what goods and services to produce, how to produce them, and how to distribute them are made based on the way things have been done in the past.

transfer payment   A payment made to someone for which no goods or services were currently produced in return. Social Security payments, unemployment insurance payments, and dividends earned from owning stock are examples of transfer payments.

underemployed workers   Those who are working part time but who would like to be working full time, or workers who have jobs that do not make the best use of their skills or training.

unemployed   According to the Bureau of Labor Statistics, someone who is in the labor force and available for work but does not have a job, and who has actively looked for a job in the past four weeks.

unemployment rate   The number of unemployed people divided by the number of people in the labor force.

unit of account   The function that money performs when it is used to express the value of something.

value-added approach to measuring GDP   Summing up the amount added to the value of products at each stage of production, instead of using the value of final goods and services.

velocity of money   How many times a dollar is spent on average during a certain time period.

BIBLIOGRAPHY

About the Fed. Federal Reserve Bank of San Francisco. Retrieved online August 2011 at http://www.frbsf.org/federalreserve/.

Barro, Robert J., and Charles J. Redlick. "Stimulus Spending Doesn't Work." *The Wall Street Journal.* 2009. Retrieved online September 2011 at http://online.wsj.com/article/SB10001424052748704471504574440723298786310.html.

Borbely, James M. U.S. Labor Market in 2008: Economy in Recession. Bureau of Labor Statistics. Retrieved online July 2011 at http://www.bls.gov/opub/mlr/2009/03/art1full.pdf.

Bureau of Economic Analysis. Gross Domestic Product (GD) Price Index. Retrieved online July 2011 and www.bea.gov/glossary/.

Bureau of Economic Analysis. Table 1.1.9 Implicit Price Deflators for Gross Domestic Product. Retrieved online July 2011 at http://www.bea.gov/national/nipaweb/.

Bureau of Economic Analysis. U.S. Department of Commerce. www.bea.gov.

Carlstrom, Charles T., and Timothy S. Fuerst. Monetary Policy in a World with Interest on Reserves. Federal Reserve Bank of Cleveland. 2010. Retrieved online September 2011 at http://www.clevelandfed.org/research/commentary/2010/2010-4.cfm.

CIA World Factbook Country Comparisons. Retrieved online June 2011 at www.cia.gov.

Conference Board. Global Business Cycle Indicators. Retrieved online July 2011 at http://www.conference-board.org/data/bcicountry.cfm?cid=1.

Congressional Budget Office. http://www.cbo.gov/.

Consumer Price Index. Bureau of Labor Statistics. Retrieved online July 2100 at http://www.bls.gov/cpi/.

Cowen, David. "The First Bank of the United States." *EH.net Encyclopedia.* Retrieved online August 2011 at http://eh.net/encyclopedia/article/cowen .banking.first_bank.us.

Crawford, Malik, and Jonathan Church, editors. CPI Detailed Report: Data for May 2011. Bureau of Labor Statistics. Retrieved online July 2011 at http://www.bls.gov/cpi/cpid1105.pdf.

"The Debt to the Penny and Who Holds It." U.S. Treasury Department. Retrieved online September 2011 at http://www.treasurydirect.gov/NP/BPDLogin?application=np.

Delong, J. Bradford. "The Reality of Economic Growth: History and Prospect." Retrieved online June 2011 at http://www.j-bradford-delong.net/macro_ online/ms/ch5/chapter_5.pdf

"Economic Crisis and Market Upheavals." *New York Times Topics.* Retrieved online September 2011 at http://topics.nytimes.com/top/reference/ timestopics/subjects/c/credit_crisis/index.html?scp=1&sq=economic%20 crisis%20&st=cse.

Economic Report of the President: 2011 Report Spreadsheet Tables. Available online, Accessed 5/2011. http://www.gpoaccess.gov/eop/.

FDIC: Who is the FDIC? Retrieved online August 2011 at http://www.fdic.gov/ about/learn/symbol/index.html.

Federal Reserve Discount Window. Retrieved online August 2011 at http://www.frbdiscountwindow.org/index.cfm.

Federal Reserve Statistical Release H.6. Money Stock Measures. Retrieved online august 2011 at http://www.federalreserve.gov/releases/h6/current/.

Gregory, Paul R., and Robert C. Stuart. *Comparing Economic Systems in the Twenty-First Century.* 7th ed. Boston: Houghton Mifflin Company, 2004.

A Guide to the National Income and Product Accounts of the United States. Bureau of Economic Analysis. Available online. Accessed May, 2011 at http://www.bea.gov/national/pdf/nipaguid.pdf.

Henderson, David R. ed. *The Concise Encyclopedia of Economics. Library of Economics and Liberty.* Retrieved online March 2012 at http://www .econlib.org/library/CEE.html

The History of Gold. The National Mining Association. Retrieved online August 2011 at http://www.nma.org/pdf/gold/gold_history.pdf.

The History of Money. The Federal Reserve Bank of Minneapolis. Retrieved online August 2011 at www.minneapolisfed.org/community_education/ teacher/history.cfm.

The History of Money. Nova. Retrieved online August 2011 at www.pbs.org/wgbh/nova/ancient/history-money.html.

An Introduction to the National Income and Product Accounts. BEA: U.S. Department of Commerce. September, 2007. Available online. Accessed April 2011 at http://www.bea.gov/scb/pdf/national/nipa/methpap/mpi1_0907.pdf.

John F. Kennedy Quotations. John F. Kennedy Presidential Library & Museum. Retrieved online June 2011 at http://www.jfklibrary.org/Research/Ready-Reference/JFK-Quotations.aspx.

"Lessons from History: Stock Market Crashes." *Learning, Earning and Investing.* New York: National Council on Economic Education, 2004.

Lucas, Robert E. "On the Mechanics of Economic Development." *Journal of Monetary Economics* 22 (1988): 3–42.

M1 Money Multiplier. Economics Research: Federal Reserve Bank of St. Louis. Retrieved online August 2011 at http://research.stlouisfed.org/fred2/series/MULT.

Monetary Policy. Board of Governors of the Federal Reserve System. Retrieved online August 2011 at http://www.federalreserve.gov/.

The NBER's Business Cycle Dating Committee. National Bureau of Economic Research. Retrieved online July 2011 at www.nber.org/cycles/recessions.html.

The NBER's Business Cycle Dating Procedure: Frequently Asked Questions. National Bureau of Economic Research. Retrieved online July 2011 at www.nber.org/cycles/recessions_faq.html.

National Income and Product Accounts, Bureau of Economic Analysis. Available online. Accessed 5/20/11 at http://www.bea.gov/national/nipaweb/TableView.asp?SelectedTable=43&FirstYear=2010&LastYear=2011&Freq=Qtr.

National Park Service: The U.S. Constitution: Second Bank of the United States. Retrieved online August 2011 at http://www.cr.nps.gov/history/online_books/butowsky2/constitution7.htm

Ownership of Federal Debt. 9/21/2011. U.S. Government Accounting Office. Retrieved online September 2011 at http://www.gao.gov/special.pubs/longterm/debt/ownership.html.

"Ownership of Federal Securities." *Treasury Bulletin.* September 2011. Retrieved online September 2011 at http://www.fms.treas.gov/bulletin/b2011_3ofs.doc.

Parker, Randall. "An Overview of the Great Depression." Posted 2.5.2010 on EH.net. Retrieved online September 2011 at http://eh.net/encyclopedia/article/parker.depression.

"Quantitative Easing Explained." *Liber8: Economic Information Newsletter.* April 2011. Federal Reserve Bank of St. Louis. Retrieved online September 2011 at http://liber8.stlouisfed.org/newsletter/2011/201104.pdf.

Real GDP 1962–2010. *Economic Report of the President* 2011. Retrieved online June 2011 at http://www.gpoaccess.gov/eop/2011/xls/ERP-2011-table2.xls.

Real GDP, Percent Change. Bureau of Economic Analysis. U.S. Department of Commerce. Retrieved online June 2011 at http://www.bea.gov/briefrm/gdp.htm.

"Senate Passes $787 Billion Stimulus Bill." CNNMoney.com. February 15, 2009. Retrieved online September 2011 at http://money.cnn.com/2009/02/13/news/economy/house_final_stimulus/index.htm.

Shim, Jae K., and Joel G. Siegel. *Dictionary of Economics.* New York: John Wiley & Sons, 1995.

"Taking Apart the Federal Budget." *Washington Post.* Retrieved online September 2011 at http://www.washingtonpost.com/wp-srv/special/politics/budget-2010/.

Timberlake, Richard H. "The Original Federal Reserve System." *The Concise Encyclopedia of Economics.* Retrieved online August 2011 at http://www.econlib.org/library/Enc/FederalReserveSystem.html.

Toscano, Paul. "The Worst Hyperinflation Situations of All Time." Retrieved online July 2011 at http://www.cnbc.com/id/41532451/The_Worst_Hyperinflation_Situations_of_All_Time?

2011 Index of Economic Freedom. Heritage Foundation. Retrieved online September 2011 at www.heritage.org/Index.

Unemployment Rate. Bureau of Labor Statistics Data. Retrieved online July 2011 at http://data.bls.gov/pdq/SurveyOutputServlet.

United Nations Statistics Division: Demographic and Social Statistics. Retrieved online June 2011 at http://unstats.un.org/unsd/demographic/products/socind/education.htm.

U.S. Business Cycle Expansions and Contractions. National Bureau of Economic Research. Retrieved online July 2011 at www.nber.org/cyclces.html.

"Zimbabwe Inflation Hits 11,200,000 Percent." CNN.com. August 19, 2008. Retrieved online July 2011 at http://edition.cnn.com/2008/BUSINESS/08/19/zimbabwe.inflation/index.html.

INDEX

Index note: Page numbers followed by *g* indicate glossary entries.